Lords to Bureaucrats

A HISTORY OF SUSSEX TOWN HALLS AND THEIR LOCAL BENEFACTORS

Stephen leVine

Loncastle South.

Copyright © 2016 Stephen le Vine.

All rights reserved. The moral right of the author has been asserted. No part of this publication may be reproduced, distributed or transmitted in any form or by any means, including photocopying, recording, or other electronic or mechanical methods, without the prior written permission of the publisher, except in the case of brief quotations embodied in critical reviews and certain other non-commercial uses permitted by copyright law.

First Published 2016
Loncastle South
5/19, Upper Avenue, Eastbourne,
East Sussex. BN21 3XR U.K.
email: loncastlesouth@yahoo.co.uk

Available from Amazon.com and other retail outlets.

Book cover design by Wolf Enterprizes U K Ltd. Eastbourne. U.K.

British Library Cataloguing in Publication Data.
A catalogue record for this book is available from the British Library.

ISBN: 099354410X
ISBN-13: 978-0-9935441-0-1

To B and my family for their support.

ACKNOWLEDGMENTS

Acknowledgements and sincere thanks are passed to all at the West and East Sussex Records offices and the various libraries throughout the county that have helped with research into this book. Also thanks to the museums in Sussex that have given useful information. With special thanks to Ruth Mariner, Ann Foxall and the many town clerks and planning officers within the county for their expert assistance. All photographs are from my collection except for page 84 kindly supplied by Adur District Council.

CONTENTS

LORDS TO BUREAUCRATS i

1 Introduction 1

    Municipal Corporations Act 1835 6

2 History 7

3 County District Hundreds 13

4 West Sussex 21

    Arundel 22

    Bognor Regis 26

        West Sussex County Council 30

    Burgess Hill 31

    Chichester 33

        West Sussex County Council 41

    Crawley 44

    Haywards Heath 48

        Mid-Sussex District Council 51

    Horsham 52

        West Sussex 60

Midhurst 61

Petworth 64

Portslade 67

Shoreham 69

    Adur District Council 72

Southwick 73

Steyning 75

Worthing 78

    West Sussex County Council 83

5 Miscellaneous West Sussex. 85

    East Grinstead 86

    Littlehampton 88

        Arun District Council 91

    Rustington 93

    Selsey 95

6 East Sussex 99

    Bexhill 100

        Rother District Council 103

    Brighton 104

Eastbourne 110

Hastings 115

Hove 120

Lewes 125

    East Sussex County Council 130

Pevensey 135

Rye 137

Seaford 140

Winchelsea 146

7 Miscellaneous East Sussex. 149

    Battle 150

    Crowborough 153

    Wealden District Council 155

    Hailsham 156

    Wealden District Council 161

    Newhaven 162

    Peacehaven 165

    Polegate 166

    Telscombe 168

Uckfield	170
Glossary	173
Bibliography	175
Index of People	183
General Index	189

1 Introduction

This book is not just about the history of Sussex or the towns we have an interest in. I have tried to provide some helpful information and background details to explain the antiquity of our county towns. There are many good books on the County and individual towns in Sussex available from the libraries or bookshops. We are concerned with the buildings and the townsfolk that supported civic society.

With modern changes to local government and the move from Town Halls to ordinary office blocks, a record of a town's municipal history is needed. We are losing knowledge and history with the passage of time and the deaths of so many local long-serving representatives of local government.

There has been a record of the county name of Sussex in ancient documents from the Saxon period although the history of human habitation in Sussex goes back to the Old Stone Age. Sussex is a small county only eighty miles long and forty miles from its northern boundaries to the sea. Originally, the land known as the Kingdom of the South Saxons changed and renamed to the Kingdom of Sussex.

The home of the South Saxons back in 477AD and one of the seven Anglo-Saxon Kingdoms, it has since been split into two counties. This has proved to be a convenient point on the South coast of England for the major Roman and later Norman invasions of Great Britain and repeated raids by the French, Danish and Spanish fleets.

After the Norman Conquest, the governance of the county subdivided into districts called **'Rapes'**. These were from the coast to the county northern boundary and dominated by a lord with a castle.

The Rapes named after the lord's estate and castle and then further divided into smaller governable areas called **'Hundreds'**.

In the eleventh century, the county was set up into the Archdeaconry of Chichester and the Archdeaconry of Lewes. With the Reform Act of 1832, both the eastern and western divisions followed the same boundaries as the archdeaconries.

Later, after the Local Government Act 1888, the county adopted the system of County Councils. This created West Sussex with the county town of Chichester made up from the Rapes of Chichester, Arundel and Bramber. Then East Sussex with its county town of Lewes made up from the Rapes of Lewes and Pevensey. Pevensey had its own corporation until 1866. The county boroughs of Brighton, Hastings and Eastbourne were the exceptions. Later, the Local Government Act that is also known as the Parish Act of 17 December 1894, the local government changed to Parish Councils, District Councils and County Councils.

It is not surprising that we have many towns in East Sussex belonging to the Cinque Ports (Quinque Portunus) Association. This dates from the eleventh century and Edward the Confessor (c1003 – 1066). These ports set up to defend the country and provide fleets to meet the military needs of the sovereigns. With their nearness to France, the port towns became targets for regular raids. In retaliation, many Sussex towns also mounted raids on the French coast.

After the Norman invasion of 1066, the ports were fortified and expanded. There were three original ports being Dover, Sandwich and Romsey, later Hastings (1155) and Hythe (1155) joined them.

Added later were the ports of Seaford (pre-1229), Pevensey, Fordwich (1050), Winchelsea (1191), and Rye (1191). Folkestone (1313/4), Feversham (1252), Lydd (the 1200s) and Terterden (1449) also joined the Association. In return for services to the State, the towns gained extra rights and advantages in local and national government. Other benefits were exemptions from tax and customs duties.

The history of expansion and then contraction of the Cinque Ports Corporation are known and there are many books on the subject.

Introduction

There have been municipal changes in the county with East Sussex and Lewes and the districts of Eastbourne, Hastings, Rother and Wealden. As well as West Sussex, Chichester, and the districts of Adur, Arun, Crawley, Horsham, Mid Sussex and Worthing. With Brighton and Hove now a city managing its own affairs. East Sussex originally included Burgess Hill, Cuckfield, and East Grinstead although Brighton and Hastings were independent county boroughs. Eastbourne also became an independent county borough in April 1911.

There were further changes in the 1972 Local Government Act when the towns of Brighton, Eastbourne and Hastings lost their independent status. They then merged under the East Sussex County Council governance.

In April 1974, boundary changes compelled East Grinstead, Haywards Heath, Burgess Hill and Cuckfield to become part of West Sussex for the first time.

Currently, East Sussex contains the boroughs of Eastbourne and Hastings and the districts of Lewes. It also embraces the Wealden district, comprising of the inland Rural Districts of Uckfield and Hailsham. Also included under the County Council governance is the Rother District Council that encompasses the coastal Borough of Bexhill and Rural District of Battle.

The East Sussex County Council held their first meeting on the 7 February 1889 in Eastbourne, electing Lord Monk Bretton, the Liberal MP for Sussex as the new chairman. He had held that position on the now defunct Local Board. After complaints from Lewes's mayor, T.H. White, all further meetings took place in Lewes. The last meeting of the council was on the 19 March 1974 when the chairman was Reginald Edwardes-Jones.

West Sussex County Council held their first meeting in January 1889 in North Street, Chichester and R.B. Willis was their first chairman. The County then only had one city, namely Chichester until 2000 when Brighton & Hove became a city.

Local government is essential for a civilised society, whether elected officials we have today or feudal Lords, landowners and town elders.

Society needs a group, town council or corporation to oversee the tasks of street lighting, cleaning and sanitation.

This would also include the local administration of the roads, education and collection of local taxes, policing, as well as judicial services.

The Town Halls are the focus of our civic society and usually the main administrative centre; they grow and expand with the prosperity of the town.

Early buildings typically housed other important sections of local government like magistrate courts, police station and prisoner cells and even in various towns, fire stations. Sometimes, a town has only had one Town Hall, when in others they have had two or three previous Town Halls, some of which still survive.

After the Lighting and Watching Act 1833, it was possible for a parish to provide a fire fighting service and make a charge against the rates they raised. Many small villages and towns in the county through the Vestry provided this service and some even supplied fire engines or other fire fighting equipment until the County Council took over these services.

Some people say the story of the Town Hall started with the 1835 Municipal Reform Act, but there were already Town Halls in the county in the older towns.

None of these earlier buildings are as impressive in style as the Victorian or Edwardian of later years.

There are small buildings, large Gothic style and modern concrete and glass buildings. In the county, many of these are listed buildings. Town Halls are in large Borough towns as well as in small towns where they have limited authority on local government.

Some Town Halls today are used for their original purpose while others have had their powers transferred to large civic or county halls. A few have changed their use to museums, private businesses or just a branch office for the local urban district. There are small towns with a mayor and larger towns that have never elected a mayor. Uniquely there is one small town, which had two mayors over ten years, but the mayors in the post only for just over two hundred days.

We have come a long way since the Lord of the Manor ruled the towns and counties.

Without the patronage of the Lords and local businessmen and their generosity of giving land and money, we may never have seen the constructing of many of our Town Halls.

Introduction

The governance has changed over the years, from one-man or family to one vote for every man or woman registered in a district. Without local government, our towns and villages would be without clean water, electricity, rubbish clearing and decent roads. In many towns, the local council or parish council set up policing and the early fire brigades and sometimes the ambulance service.

There would be chaos and only the wealthy could have a decent standard of living and the poor would be living in a squalid lawless society.

Today the idea of the Town Hall can be confusing. Now with the constraints on modern government and financial limits, many Town Hall buildings are marriage halls or entertainment establishments. With the changeover of some of the old buildings into private homes or restaurants, this forced municipal staff into modern office blocks.

National government wants to take on more responsibilities and the idea of the central local hub for community affairs is disappearing. There are not the benefactors these days with the vision or local pride who want to promote their community and local district.

For more detailed background and references of the early government by manorial boroughs, the Vestry and Quarter Sessions, see the books by Sidney and Beatrice Webb. They are The English Local Government – The Manor and the Borough and The Parish and the County and are well worth reading.

* * * * * * * * *

Municipal Corporations Act 1835

Some of the main points from the act:

Any male person of full age having occupied any house, shop within the borough during the year and the whole of the two preceding years could vote. Additionally they could hold the offices of Burgess of the Borough and be members of the Corporate.

Every person in the Borough had the right to trade in any shop or business subject to custom or Bye-Laws.

The elected councillors were in office for three years subject to one-third of the council holding annual elections.

One person should be selected mayor for a period of one year.

Aldermen and Councillors should be chosen to run the Borough.

All closed corporations were required to be abolished.

Accounts are to be audited and a town clerk and treasurer were needed to be appointed.

Councils could take over the duties of social improvement like street cleaning, lighting, water supply and similar activities.

An appointment needed for a Watch Committee and police force.

Any town or city that did not have a council could apply for incorporation.

2 History

The term 'Town Hall' has been a general one, often applied without regard to whether the building serves or served a town or a city. The Oxford English Dictionary sums up the generic terms:

Town Hall: "A large hall used for the transaction of the public business of a town, the holding of a court of justice, assemblies, entertainments, etc.; the great hall of the town-house or municipal building; now very commonly applied to the whole building"

Since ancient times, tribal chiefs and elders have arranged within their village a special place for meetings and discussions on community life. This was where they debated and resolved disputes

Throughout the country discoveries in Celtic settlements have found remains of long and roundhouses with artefacts. The Anglo-Saxons used to hold town meetings to decreed common law and appoint various officials. The Saxon system was lost with the introduction of the manorial Court Leet. In ancient Rome, they used sizeable halls called basilicas for meeting places, administration of justice, and trade.

There was a scheme in Sussex known as **'Rape'**, which was only a geographical division of the county.

Originally, in six areas, all of which had coastal access and a castle (Chichester, Arundel, Bramber, Lewes, Pevensey and Hastings).

These were then further split into **'Hundreds'**, that were for administrative and judicial purposes. When introduced by the Saxons between 613 and 1017, a hundred had enough land to sustain about one hundred households. A 'hundred-man' or 'hundred elder' headed this.

He was responsible for administration, justice, and supplying military troops to the lord of the manor or to the monarch. By the tenth century, the selection for the office was from a few privileged and high-status families. The barony controlled the Rapes and the towns were controlled by the manor of the boroughs. Within each hundred there was a meeting place where the men of the hundred discussed local issues, and judicial trials took place. Hundreds further divided; larger or more populous hundreds split into divisions (or in Sussex, half hundreds). With the forming of county courts in 1867, the importance of the hundred courts declined and they lost most of their powers.

During the Early Medieval period, a single large open chamber, the hall was the main living quarters of the home of a feudal lord. There the lord lived with his family and retinue, ate, slept and administered rule and justice. Activities in the hall played an essential role in the feudal manor, the administrative entity of society. As manorial homes developed into manor houses, castles, and palaces, the hall, or 'great hall' as it was often termed, remained an essential unit within the architectural complex.

The first Parliament as we know it was formed in 1295 by King Edward I (1272 - 1307). This was some years after the Simon de Montfort's parliaments of 1264 - 1265. This brought about many changes in the way of governance of Britain. The name given to the first house was the House of Commons. Later there was a second chamber set up in the reign of Edward III (1327 - 1377) for Bishops and Barons and known as the House of Lords.

From the 1290s, it was usual for large buildings to comprise a large meeting hall and many administrative chambers. In larger towns, tall towers topped buildings with timepieces by which the people of the town could regulate their lives. These buildings had facilities for the storage of documents and references that refer to the city's administration. These features: a hall, a tower and a clock, as well as administrative chambers and an archive, became the standard features of Town Halls in larger towns across England and Europe.

One of the grandest examples of the medieval era was Brussels Town Hall of the fifteenth century. This building with its ninety-six metre (three hundred and fifteen feet) tower was a model for the nineteenth century Town Halls across Europe.

The Lord of the Manor had a duty to offer his poor, shelter and food if needed. As the church started to receive new responsibilities, they arranged relief and support to the poor. The Poor Relief Act of 1601 allowed the Vestry to levy a 'poor rate' and this became the foundation of our modern rating system.

The first steps to democracy and the people given a stake in political life started in 1832 with the Reform Bill. The Poor Law Act of 1834, known as the New Poor Law, followed this. The Municipal Corporation Act the following year set up one hundred and seventy-eight municipal corporations in the country. This Act provided for local elections by male ratepayers of age, that were residents in a town for three years. If any other town wished to receive a charter of incorporation, they would have to apply and usually had a long wait to resolve the matter.

It would take until 1918 that women over the age of thirty could vote and 1928 until all women over the age of 21 years had the vote.

Many towns and villages had a volunteer fire service and limited equipment. It was not until after the Watching and Lighting Act 1835 that it became a legal requirement for local councils to provide a fire service.

Later the Towns Police Act Clause Act 1847 allowed the purchase of fire appliances and payment for the crews out of the Poor Rates. In September 1941, national government set up the National Fire Service. This brought town and municipal fire brigades under the nationwide organisation. It was not until after World War 2 that in 1946 the government agreed to return control to the County Councils.

By convention, until the mid-nineteenth century, a single large open chamber (or hall) formed an integral part of the building housing the council. Theses council meetings and other significant events took place in the hall. This large chamber, the 'Town Hall', has become synonymous with the whole building, and the administrative body housed in it.

Major changes were happening.

The passage of the Local Government Act of 1894 created Urban and Rural District Councils to replace the Sanitary Districts and Poor Law Unions. This brought local government to the people. Changes in 1974 superseded these Acts. The year 1894 saw the creating of the Civil Parish Councils and over the years, the boundaries of these parishes have seen many changes.

Parishes are the first and lowest form of local government and every four years they hold members' elections. They took over the duties of the Vestry committees, a system that had been in existence since the eighth century. Over the years, with changes in local government, some parishes have grown and some blended into larger parishes.

After the Local Government Act of 1972, there were changes so any parish could have a town council and the area called a town. Urban Boroughs and Urban Districts ended and many Rural Boroughs became parishes.

The creation of Successor parishes, three hundred after the 1972 Act, had the same boundaries as before and could call themselves towns. If they wished, they could elect a town mayor, but not all chose this option.

The 1997 Local Government and Rating Act made it possible for a district council to create a new parish council if there was a demand in the area for this.

With the coming of the Industrial Revolution, the modern concept of the Town Hall advanced with the developing local and regional governments. Cities and towns, governed by a group of elected or chosen representatives, rather than by a lord or princely ruler, needed a place for their council to meet. During the nineteenth century, Town Hall buildings often included reading rooms. These were to provide free education to the public. It eventually became normal for the town or city council to set up and maintain a library as part of its service to the community.

The grand chamber or meeting place, the 'Town Hall' itself, became a place for receptions, banquets, balls and public entertainment. Other services often housed in the same building have been magistrate courts or police stations.

Town Halls, during the nineteenth century, were resplendent buildings often equipped with large pipe organs and elaborate stained-glass windows. This reflected the new prosperity of the town.

History

In the twentieth century, Town Halls, as venues, have served the public as places for public civic notices, voting, academic examinations, vaccinations, blood donor sessions, and relief in times of disaster. As well as a focal point in emergencies, the building hosted the more usual civic roles, festivities, and entertainments.

With expanding towns and cities, local councils have tended increasingly to remove administrative tasks into modern offices. When designing and building new properties, the offices of local government and ideas and roles as administrative council offices sometimes can be confused.

In modern days, the local government may strive to use the Town Hall building to promote and improve the quality of life of the community. Often, Town Halls serve not only as buildings for government functions but also have facilities for various civic and cultural activities. These may include art shows, stage performances, displays and festivals as well as hiring out rooms to generate extra income for the council. Often the designs of modern Town Halls or Civic Centres have great variety and flexibility of purpose in mind.

During World War 2, many Town Halls were the centre of the Civil Defence services. Later with the Cold War, it became usual to house nuclear and emergency centres in the basement of buildings of the larger council properties.

There are still some old Town Hall buildings in use today, some as libraries with others as museums or private businesses. Others still house council offices, although the power has been transferred to large Civic Halls and their use is much a branch office.

As symbols of local government, City and Town Halls can have a distinctive and grandiose architecture. The buildings may have great historical significance as many famous architects have designed buildings in the larger towns and cities and some now are protected listed structures.

So, we have moved from the lord of the manor, holding courts of justice for his tenants, dealing with disputes and other matters that affected economic life and The King's Court or Court Leet. Who also dealt with the criminal as well as civic matters. Now we have locally elected and accountable councils that govern the district.

With the Representation of the People Act 1867, every male householder over the age of twenty-one years could vote in secret for his local councillors. There had been much buying of votes and corruption in the old boroughs.

The new act helped ordinary people, or as we said before, men to have a say and control in local affairs.

We had some large towns in the county served by good mail coach links, but not all the roads were safe or comfortable to travel on. In the winter and bad weather, many roads became impassable and the coaches became bogged down.

With the coming of the railway in the nineteenth century, everything changed and the county started to prosper. Rail links from the larger towns and London to the coast enabled wealthy patrons and entrepreneurs to visit and buy properties. Now, day-trippers could also visit the seaside resorts.

It did not take the local landowners long to develop their towns and cater for the new influx of visitors. Goods moved around more easily and the markets and ports benefited from these changes.

* * * * * * * * *

3 County District Hundreds

West Sussex

Rape of Bramber	Parish
Brightford (Worthing)	Broadwater, Clapham, Durrington, Findon, Heene, Lancing, Sompting.
Burbeach	Ifield, Lower Breeding, Upper Breeding.
East Easwrith	Itchingfield, Sullington, Thakeham, Warminghurst.
Fishergaye	Kingston-by-Sea, New Shoreham, Old Shoreham, Southwick.
Patching	Patching.
Singlecross	Horsham, Nuthurst, Rusper, Warnham.
Steyning (Bramber)	Bramber, Buttolphs, Coombes, Steyning, Washington, Wiston.
Tarring	West Tarring.
Tipnoak	Albourne, Henfield, Woodmancote.
W.Grinstead	Ashington, Ashurst, Shipley, W.Grinstead.
Windham & Ewhurst	Cowfold, Shermanbury.

Lords to Bureaucrats

Rape of Arundel	Parish
Arundel	Arundel.
Avisford	Barnham, Binstead, Climping, Eastergate, Felpham, Ford, Madehurst, Middleton, Tortingham, Walberton, Yapton.
Bury	Bignor, Coates, Cold Waltham, Fittleworth, Hardham, Houghton, Wisborough Green.
Poling (Littlehampton)	Angmering, Burpham, East Preston, Ferring, Goring, Leominster, Poling, Littlehampton, Rustington, Warningcamp.
Rotherbridge (Petworth)	Barlavington, Burton, Duncton, Egdean, Kirdford, Lurgashall, North Chapel, Petworth, Stopham, Sutton, Tillington, East Lavington.
West Easwrith	Amberley, Billingshurst, Greatham, Parham, Pulborough, Rackham, Slinfold, Rudgwick, Storrington, West Chiltington, Wiggonholt.

County District Hundreds

Rape of Chichester	Parish
Aldwick (Lavant)	East Lavant, Pagham, Slindon, South Bersted, Tangmere, West Lavington.
Bosham	Bosham, Chidham, Funtington, West Stoke, West Thorney.
Box & Stockbridge	Aldingbourn, Appledram, Boxgrove, Donnington, Eartham, Hunston, Merston, New Fishbourne, North Mundham, Oving, Rumboldswyke, Upper Waltham, Westhampnett.
Dumpford	Chithurst, Didling, Elsted, Harting, Rogate, Terwick, Treyford, Trotton.
Easebourne (Midhurst)	Bepton, Cocking, Easebourne, Furnhurst, Graffham, Heyshott, Iping, Linch, Linchmere, Lodsworth, Midhurst, Ambersham, Selham, Stedham, Woolbeding.
Manhood (Silsey)	Birdham, Earnley, East Wittering, Selsey, Sidlesham, West Itchenor, West Wittering.
Westbourne & Singleton	Binderton, Compton, East Dean, East Marden, Mid Lavant, North Marden, Racton, Singleton, Stoughton, Upper Marden, Westbourne, West Dean.

Lords to Bureaucrats

County District Hundreds:

East Sussex

Rape of Hastings	Parish
Baldslow	Crowhurst, Hollington, St.Leonards, Ore, St.Mary-in-the-Castle, Westfield.
Battle	Battle, Whatlington.
Bexhill	Bexhill.
Foxearle	Ashburnham, Hurstmonceaux, Wartling.
Goldspur	Beckley, Broomhill(part), Guildford, Iden, Peasmarsh, Playden.
Gostrow	Brede, Udimore.
Guestling	Fairlight, Guestling, Icklesham, Pett.
Hawkesborough	Burwash(part), Heathfield, Warbleton.
Henhurst	Burwash(part), Etchingham, Salehurst.
Netherfield	Brightling, Dallington, Mountfield, Penhurst.
Ninfield	Catsfield, Hooe, Ninfield.
Shagswell	Burwash(part), Ticehurst.
Staple	Bodiam, Ewhurst, Northiam, Sedlescombe.

County District Hundreds

Rape of Pevensey	Parish
Alciston	Alciston, Alfriston, Lullington.
Bishopstone	Bishopstone, Denton.
Danehill Horsted	Horsted Keynes, Selmeston & Tarring, Neville, Or East Tarring.
Dill (Hailsham)	Hailsham, Hellingley.
Eastbourne	Borne (Eastbourne)
East Grinstead	East Grinstead.
Flexborough	East Blatchington, Seaford, South Heighton.
Hartfield	Hartfield, Withyham.
Lindfield	Burleigh Arches.
Longbridge	Arlington, Berwick, Folkington, Littlington, Wilmington.
Loxfield Camden	Lamberhurst(part), Mayfield, Wadhurst.
Loxfield Dorset	Buxted, Framfield, Isfield, Uckfield.
Pevensey Lowey	Pevensey, Westham.
Ringmer	Glynde, Ringmer, South Malling, Stanmer.
Rotherfield	Frant, Rotherfield.
Rushmonden	Fletching, Little Horstead, Maresfield.
Shiplake	Chalvington, Chiddingly, East Hoathly, Laughton, Ripe, Waldron.
Totnor	Beddingham, West Firle.
Willingdon	East Dean, Friston, Jevington, West Dean, Willingdon.

Lords to Bureaucrats

Rape of Lewes	Parish
Barcombe	Barcombe, Hamsey, Newick.
Buttinghill (Cuckfield)	Ardingly, Balcombe, Bolney, Clayton, Crawley, Cuckfield, Hurstpierpoint, Keymer, Slaugham, Twineham, West Hoathley, Worth.
Dean	Patcham.
Fishergate	Aldrington, Hangleton, Portslade.
Holmstrow	Newhaven, Piddinghoe, Rodmell, Southease, Telscombe.
Poynings	Edburton (part), Newtimber, Poynings, Pycombe.
Preston	Hove, Preston.
Street	Chailey, Ditchling, East Chiltington, Plumpton, Street, Westmeston, Wivelsfield.
Swanborough	Iford, Kingston nr Lewes.
Whalesbone (Welesmere)	West Blatchungton, Brighton.
Youngsmere	Palmer, Ovingdean, Rottingdean.

County District Hundreds

1974 changes after Local Government Act of 1972.

East Sussex

District	Successor
Battle Rural District	Rother
Bexhill Borough	Rother
Burgess Hill Urban District	Mid Sussex
Chailey Rural District	Lewes
Cuckfield Rural District	Mid Sussex, Crawley
Cuckfield Urban District	Mid Sussex
East Grinstead Urban District	Mid Sussex
Hailsham Rural District	Wealden
Hove Borough	Hove
Lewes Borough	Lewes
Newhaven Urban District	Lewes
Portslade-by-Sea Urban District	Hove
Rye Borough	Rother
Seaford Urban District	Lewes
Uckfield Rural District	Wealden

Brighton, Eastbourne and Hastings were county boroughs.

Lords to Bureaucrats

West Sussex

District	Successor
Arundel Borough	Arun
Bognor Regis Urban District	Arun
Chanctonbury Rural District	Horsham
Chichester Borough	Chichester
Chichester Rural District	Arun, Chichester
Crawley Urban District	Crawley
Horsham Rural District	Horsham
Horsham Urban District	Horsham
Littlehampton Urban District	Arun
Midhurst Rural District	Chichester
Petworth Rural District	Chichester
Shoreham-by-Sea Urban District	Adur
Southwick Urban District	Adur
Worthing Borough	Worthing
Worthing Rural District	Adur, Arun

There were no county boroughs

* * * * * * * * *

4 West Sussex

It was 1888 when we saw the formation of the counties of East Sussex and West Sussex along the traditional boundaries of the old Kingdom of Sussex. The previous county had traditionally divided into units called **'rapes'** but the County Councils superseded these. The original meeting of the West Sussex Council was in January 1889 and their first full business meeting took place in North Street, Chichester on 1 April 1889.

Arundel

10, Maltravers Street, Arundel, West Sussex BN18 9AP

First mentioned in 877 when in his will King Alfred (871 – 99) left the town by the river Arun to his nephew AEthelm. By the time of the Domesday Book 1086, Arundel was a thriving market town and port in the Rape of Arundel and Hundred of Avisford. The town had its own borough and bailiffs from 1254 and the first recorded mayor was Richard Dodins in 1280.

The castle in the town was built in 1067 by Roger de Montgomery originally in wood but later rebuilt in stone. It was in 1285 that the town and Richard FitzAlan, the Earl of Arundel was granted an annual fair and the town has been hosting weekly markets since at least 1086. In 1338, disaster struck and a fire destroyed half of the town, but with requests for government aid, the town was soon on the road to recovery. It grew and by the early eighteenth century, Arundel had breweries and a thriving timber trade. There was also a small shipbuilding industry in the town from 1579 until the early nineteenth century.

Queen Elizabeth I (1558 – 1603) on the 22 June 1586 granted the Charter of Incorporation to Arundel. This was when Thomas Bowler was mayor.

After the 1785 Arundel Act of Parliament, an improvement commission was set up to run the town's affairs.

The Municipal Corporations Act under the borough reforms in 1835 replaced this.

There was The Court House or sometimes-called Town House, in Market Street with an open ground floor used as a shop. The borough courts, parliamentary elections and occasionally the Quarter Sessions used the upper floor. By 1692, the corporation had neglected the building and demolished it in 1741 as it had become dilapidated. Then for some years, borough business transferred to a part of the Fitzalan chapel annexe at the parish church. Known locally as the schoolhouse, but by 1793 renamed the Court House. The town council gave up the use of the building in 1848.

After the reform of the borough in 1835, Bernard Howard, the twelfth Duke of Norfolk wanting the return of the schoolhouse erected a New Town Hall. The building designed by Robert Abraham and situated in Market Street that is now named Maltravers Street. Completion was in 1836 at a cost of nine thousand pounds.

The mayor of the new Town Council in 1836 when the new Municipal Corporation Act came into force was Arthur Atherley (1772 – 1844). The main chamber in the Town Hall, the Atherley Chamber honours his service to the community.

The building has a flint and Fittleworth sandstone façade with red and grey brick basement and foundations with a ground floor arcade. The entrance has fine Norman style vaulted ceilings and the building has two storeys with flanking towers in the Norman style. One of the towers is named the Flag Tower and the other the Constable's Tower. The main hall was fifty feet by thirty feet and twenty-three feet high. There are large stone fireplaces at each end of the room with a large, gas-lit chandelier in the centre of the room.

The chandelier that was presented in 1861 by the Rt. Hon Edward Howard MP is still in use today. In the chamber is a list of all previous mayors of the town from 1539 and Thomas Crane until the present day.

Since the 5 June 1969, the building has been Grade II listed.

In September 1995, workers discovered that the Atherley Chamber had extensive dry rot, wet rot and death-watch beetle.

Commissioned to carry out the work of major repairs was Chris Robbins, the senior Building Surveyor of West Sussex. The rebuild entailed repairs to almost all of the upper part of the building. Finally, on the 10 May 1996, the room reopened after seven months of renovation.

In the years 1829 – 1830, the parish had their own fire engines until the borough police took over responsibility in 1836. By 1902, the council took charge of the service. The town's Volunteer Fire Brigade and later the council service were housed in the Town Hall from about 1890 until 1944. Originally with their manual fire engine, handcart and horses at the back of the Town Hall.

The building at the rear had three rooms; one for the engine and cart, one for the groom and the end room housed the horses. After they moved in the 1930s to River Road, the police garaged their cars in the building and yard. In the basement of the Town Hall were three cells (which are reputed to still have ghosts of former inmates in residence) and was used by the county police from 1844 until 1911.

Between 1836 and 1889, the town had its own Borough police force of originally three men with a jurisdiction of a two-mile radius of Arundel. Later they were absorbed into the county force. A local ambulance service and their transport, a covered hand pulled wheeled cart was originally stored in the Town Hall. From 1885, the St John Ambulance Brigade managed this service. A major change came in 1930 when the Government announced proposals to reorganise local government in England and Wales, which included the transfer of responsibilities for the ambulance service to the county councils.

A railway station opened in 1846 at Lyminster some 3km away and this became known as Arundel Station. Later a new station opened in August 1863 on the eastern side of the town.

Arundel Gas Light and Coke Co, in 1838 first installed gaslights in the town. Later the Bognor Gas and Electricity Co, in 1938 supplied electricity for all residents and electric street lighting was introduced in 1964.

Lillian May Holmes presented a new courthouse to the council in 1957, which was built behind the Town Hall. The main rooms named the Holmes Chamber in memory of the Holmes family that had served the council for two hundred years as mayors and town clerks. James Holmes was the first family member to serve as mayor in 1752.

The room, just over seven and a half metres wide, by ten metres long, is now used as the council chamber. The chamber is panelled in handcrafted American black walnut and was used daily as a Magistrates' Court up to December 2001.

The town remained a borough until 1974 when it became part of the Arun district. The council held on to the title mayor, and the chairman of the successor parish council retained this title. During 1974, the mayor was William Jupp Redman.

In March 1964, the Arundel Museum opened in the old police cells of the Town Hall, before moving in 1977 into redundant offices of the Borough Council at 61 High Street. The Arundel Museum Society then became a registered charity. They stayed in the High Street until 2007 when Arundel District Council sold the building.

With local support and architect, Graham Whitehouse, there was an agreement to find new premises. It was estimated that £1.5m was needed. Construction of the new museum began in early 2012.

This was with the help of locally raised funds, Heritage Lottery Funding and a grant from Arun District Council. The Duke of Norfolk opened the museum on the 24 June 2013. The new building is opposite the castle's main entrance and is now a favourite visitor attraction in the town.

In 2008, Arun District Council claimed that they owned the Town Hall. However, after a lengthy legal battle, it was confirmed that Arundel Town Council was the legitimate owner of the Town Hall, having in their possession a document dated 5 April 1976. The document, from the chief executive to the then Arundel town clerk, informing him, the finance and general purposes and land subcommittee of the council stated:

"have decided that as the ownership of the Town Hall is vested in Arundel Town Council, the Arun District Council should cease to have any direct involvement in or responsibility for the running of these premises with effect from April 1, 1976."

It was not until late in 2010 the Town Council could finally register their ownership with HM Land Registry.

The yard by the side and rear of the Town Hall, some thirty-five feet wide by eighty feet long, that housed the fire brigade, is now in dispute.

Arun Council wishes to sell the land for redevelopment.

The mayor and the Town Council, wishing to hold on to this yard, in September 2013 put in an offer to buy the land. This matter is still unresolved.

In April 2014, the Town Council agreed to renovate the East elevation of the first floor of the Town Hall. The estimated cost of the works was twelve hundred pounds. Also needed, repair works for the council chambers at an estimate of five thousand pounds. There are also plans for works by Tunmore Design and Build of Littlehampton on the Town Hall terrace of nearly £16.5k. July 2015 saw a further £6k allocated for repairs to the leaking roof of the Town Hall.

Arun District Council now only has offices in the Civic Centre in Littlehampton and Bognor Town Hall.

Bognor Regis

Old Town Hall,
68, High Street, Bognor Regis, West Sussex.

The town's history can be traced back to AD 680 when it was known as 'Bucgan ora' (Bucge's Shore) but the name of the town has changed over the centuries. Known in 1275 as 'Buggenore' but by 1405, its name changed to 'Bogenor'.

Later in the eighteenth century, Sir Richard Hotham a London businessman renamed the town as Hothampton. After Sir Richard's death on the 13 March 1799, there was an agreement for the new name of Bognor. Following a visit from King George V (1910 – 1936) in 1928 and representation from the town council, in 1929 the council received permission to use the title 'Regis' (of the King) in the town's name.

Originally, a small village of farmers and fishermen, it has transformed into a thriving seaside town. The town in the Rape of Chichester and the Hundred of Aldwick owes its existence to Sir Richard Hotham. Sir Richard who was born in York on the 5 October 1722 and knighted in 1769. He moved to London, undertook an apprenticeship and traded as a hatter. As he prospered, he became a shipowner and builder. Later engaged in politics, he became a magistrate and then Sheriff of Surrey. In 1780 he was elected the MP for Southwark.

To improve his failing health, he moved to Bognor and invested in land. He started to develop the town in 1784 - 1799 and invested sixty thousand pounds to turn the town into a popular seaside resort. He became known as Lord of the Manor of Aldwick and continued to build houses and a hotel on the seafront.

Bognor railway station opened in June 1864 and that helped to attract wealthy Victorians into the area. There had been a previous station one mile west of the town that opened in June 1846 but this had closed in 1864.

By 1822, after an Act of Parliament, the first Town Council came into office with the appointment of Commissioners and Richard Daly as their first clerk. They had their offices at 31 High Street that they shared with other businesses. The Commissioners also used a building in 7, Hothampton Place between 1837 and 1871. Later they moved to the Assembly Rooms in 2 Sudley Road. W.K. Wonham a local builder erected this in 1837 and they stayed in the building until they moved to the New Town Hall.

Between the years 1866 and 1894, the Local Board controlled the town's affairs. They held this position until the forming of the Bognor Urban District Council in 1894 when local government reformed under the new Local Government Act of that year. Their first chairman was A.T. Long. The year 1867 saw the first police station in the town in Dorset Gardens and in 1873 the forming of a volunteer fire brigade complete with a manual fire pump.

In 1885, there was a decision to run an ambulance service with the help of the Red Cross Ambulance volunteers. The funds were raised for the 'ambulance van'; an arrangement, then made and by 1897 it was stored at the Town Hall. Patients wishing to use the service had to pay. The fees were two shillings a mile with a minimum charge of five shillings for journeys within the council district. There was a charge of five shillings a mile for transport to Chichester Infirmary with a minimum fee of ten and sixpence.

In the 1880s, the Jubilee School on the North side of the High Street, built in 1817, closed. The council's plan was to demolish the building and build a Town Hall. However, due to the high costs, this did not happen.

Mr Stringfellow, the Council surveyor, converted the building, which he managed to complete for five hundred pounds.

It opened as the Town Hall in 1882.

The building was in continuous use by the Council up to 1920s when the construction of the New Town Hall was completed.

In 1927, the council sold the original Town Hall for five thousand pounds to the Southdown Motor Company. With plans for modernization, they later demolished the old building.

The town is renowned for Billy Butlin's first amusement park in Southern England that in 1932 was constructed on the site of the Olympian Gardens. This site had once been a coal yard at the end of Lennox Street. The area boarded in and roofed, became the Olympic Gardens at the beginning of the twentieth century. Later in 1959 - 1960 the company built a new holiday camp at the East end of the promenade. This cost £2.5m. There were further developments by the firm who built in 2005, a new £10m hotel. Two more hotels followed this in 2009 and 2012.

Clarence Road, Bognor Regis, West Sussex PO21 1LD

It was in 1929 that saw the town granted the Royal accolade of Regis and the Town Council decided that they needed a New Town Hall. There was a competition and the architect chosen was Charles Cowles-Voysey.

The builder a local company, H.W. Seymour presented a tender for £18,000 5s 5d. This was accepted and work started on the new three storey, neo-Georgian style building.

On the 22 May 1929, Rev. Canon A.J. Sacre JP, Joseph Jubb and William Grice laid two foundation stones for the new building. A formal opening was on the 6 October 1929.

Mrs E Sacre performed the official opening ceremony on 11 October 1930. A picture of the town's creator, Sir Richard Hotham, is now proudly displayed in the Town Hall.

The Town Hall is in neo-Georgian style. It has good quality detailing by John Bower, in yellow Flemish bond brickwork with a hipped pantile roof. The building has fine Brown brick and stone dressing and a recently built central wooden clock tower topped with a copper domed cupola.

The three-storey building has a first-rate, oak-panelled, Council Chamber on the first floor. There is a twentieth-century flat-roofed extension on the East side. Since the 24 January 2003, the building has a Grade II listing.

During World War 2, they used the Town Hall as an air raid shelter that could house twenty-two people. There was a wartime airfield (ALG), part of Operation Hadrian, in North Bersted, and from 1942 mainly manned by Norwegian pilots and support staff. This was one of seven small airfields built in Sussex and each had two runways and up to fifty aircraft. September 1945 saw the closure of the airfield.

With the Government reorganisation in 1974, Bognor Regis merged with Littlehampton and Arundel to create the Arun District Council. Afterwards, in 1985, the Bognor Regis Town Council was set up. Mrs Pat Stinchcombe was the town's first mayor.

In 1994 on 13 August, the town was a victim of an IRA bombing, but fortunately, there were no injuries to people only damage to fifteen shops.

The Town Council decided to mark the Millennium with a timepiece on the Town Hall, as this was long overdue. In March 2000, they finally installed the new clock. This is set in a fine central wooden clock tower, with an impressive clock face and curved pediment over four Roman Doric columns. Then topped with a copper dome and finial.

Smith of Derby, founded in 1856, supplied the north-facing clock. It has a five-feet diameter skeleton dial with a centre star.

Later in November 2012, there was an agreement to install another clock on the southern face of the clock tower, after former town councillor Ken Scutt suggested the idea.

The total cost of this addition was less than four thousand pounds with Mr Scutt contributing two thousand pounds to the costs.

There had been much discussion back in 1984 and again in 2002 to demolish the Town Hall, owned by Arun District Council, and to build residential properties. Thankfully, since January 2003, the building has received a Grade II listing and is safe from developers.

In 2008, Arun District Council arranged for the major refurbishment of the Town Hall at a cost of twenty-six thousand pounds. This was in time for the eightieth anniversary of the foundation stone laying.

Arun District Council has offices in the Town Hall, as well as in Littlehampton.

West Sussex County Council

Durban House, Durban Road, Bognor Regis,
West Sussex, PO22 9RE

The council also has a presence in the town at Durban House in Durban Road. This is an ordinary two storey white rendered building with large glass entrance foyer.

West Sussex County Council bought the building and lands in February 2003 for £1,253,000.

Burgess Hill

96, Church Walk, Burgess Hill, West Sussex RH15 9AS

The town was in the Rape of Lewes and the Hundred of Butting Hill. It grew out of the ancient parishes of Clayton, Ditchling and Keymer and was dependent on agriculture. Brick making has been recorded since 1480 as well as an annual sheep fair that dates from 1342. As this was the first sheep and lamb fair of the year held in Sussex it was always busy. The fair always met on the 24 June, St John the Baptist day, with the last lamb and sheep fair held in 1913.

Local residents shared between farmers, the common land known as St John's Common between 1828 and 1855. This arrangement allowed the brick and tile industry to expand and prosper. The land had been unsuitable for farming but was clay-rich with Wealden clay and suitable for the brick and tile making industry. The town from 1830 until the 1930s was renowned for its busy brick, tile, and pottery making works and the manufacture of handmade roof tiles carry on to this day. This tradition can trace its history back to the fifteenth century.

With the arrival of the railway on 21 September 1841, the town's fortune changed.

Although the first railway station closed in October 1843, because of lack of business, a new station opened the following year on the 1 May.

Originally known as St John's Common, the village of small farms and buildings around the common land of the same name in 1879 elected to govern the expanding village. Leading businessmen of the village formed a Local Board of twelve members. They then agreed to rename the village Burgess Hill after the prominent local Burgeys family and possibly a local farm named Burgeyshill Land.

Their first meeting was at the Railway Hotel on the 7 November, when General Dickinson became their chairman. All further meetings were at the Institute until the move to Church Road offices (1882 – 1894). The Local Board found a site owned by J. Meads for their new offices and arranged for W. Downer to begin work. By September 1882, there were offices, a boardroom and a surveyor's house all completed for nine hundred and forty pounds. Behind the building, at a cost of about sixty pounds, he built a shed to house the town's fire engine (1882 – 1959).

By 1894, the newly formed Burgess Hill Urban District Council (1894 – 1974) was providing local authority services from the offices in Church Road and their first elected chairman was A.P. Scrase.

Local subscribers originally funded the fire brigade, the Burgess Hill and District Volunteer Fire Brigade until 1939. Then the District Council took over responsibility for its administration. During the war, the service was part of the National Fire Service but later merged into the East Sussex Fire Brigade in April 1948. This changed after the boundary changes of 1974.

The Police Station erected in 1890 was just next-door until their move in 1968 to The Brow. Following this, the council built new fire and ambulance stations in The Brow, on the grounds of an old tile works factory.

Originally, governed by East Sussex, because of local government reorganisation and the Local Government Act 1972, the town's status has changed. The county borders changed and the town is now in West Sussex. The newly formed Mid Sussex District Council took over many of the old Urban District Council duties.

In addition, set up in April 1974, was the Burgess Hill Town Council with the status of a parish council. Later in 2006, the Burgess Hill standing of the town changed officially to Town Council. The first elected mayor in 2001 was Chris Thomas-Atkin. In May 2014, Cllr Anne Jones MBE held this office.

Burgess Hill Town Council has occupied the building at Church Walk, the old Gas Board showroom, since their move from Church Road. The Rt. Hon. Paddy Ashdown, the then Liberal Democrat leader, officially opened the new offices on the 11 November 1996. The council is still resident in this building.

Chichester

The town was in the Rape of Chichester and Hundred of Box and Stockbridge, a municipal borough and market town. Known anciently as 'Cissan-ceaster' the fortress of Cissa, this old Roman city was to become head of the petty sessional division and county court district.

This was an old town when King Edgar (943 – 975) established a mint in 967 and the town has significant fifth century and Roman roots. It has had a cathedral since 1075 after the move from Selsey and once was a thriving port. King Stephen (1097 - 1154) granted a charter to the town and the town became incorporated in 1213. The first known mayor, Emery De Rouen (1239-1242), was appointed in 1239, although there could have been earlier appointments to the position.

The town's governors have used many buildings and some shared their use with courts and other local councils. The Corporation used a building on North Street, number sixty-four, by the church of St Peter the Less (now demolished), for council meetings. This was in use between the years 1300 – 1541 in the building known as the Gildhall or Town Hall. The building had gone by 1548 and described in old records as *"void plot where old Town Hall stood"*. Chichester was a closed Corporation until 1685 when James II (1633 – 1701) granted a new Charter.

With further changes in 1836, after the Corporation Reform Act 1835, elections took place on 1 January 1836 for a new council. The newly elected mayor was Henry Co who was then succeeded by Thomas Howe Clarke.

Unlike today, the voting was held in the Council Chamber and the results were available on a minute-to-minute basis.

By March 1847, the railway had reached the city and the first railway station opened.

After the Local Government Act 1888, Chichester became the county town of West Sussex. Again, after government reforms in 1933 the Chichester Rural District Council was set up. Later, after the Local Government Act 1972 and the reorganisations, the Chichester District Council replaced the rural council on 1 April 1974. The new council incorporated the municipal borough of Chichester and Rural Districts of Midhurst, Petworth and part of the Chichester Rural District.

Chancel of the Church of the Grey Friars,
Priory Road, Chichester, West Sussex PO19 1NS

George E Tullett was the mayor at this time. The local council lost many powers but kept the title of City Council and the Mayoralty.

After 1538, when Henry VIII (1491 – 1547) closed the friaries, the Grey Friary was demolished.

The church, which was eighty-two feet long by thirty-one feet wide and forty-two feet high, survived.

Henry VIII granted the castle grounds and chapel of 1282 to the town in November 1541. This was where the Common Council of the Corporation met and it became known as the Gildhall. In addition, this is where the Mayor's Court sat every Monday, with the Quarter Sessions also held in the building. The remainder of the site was then first leased to John Knott in 1543 and then to others.

Later the fifth Duke of Richmond bought the freehold in 1854 from the council for four thousand pounds. In 1918, the Duke's successor presented the freehold to the City. On the 5 July 1950, the Chancel received a Grade I listing.

For some time the council was meeting in two buildings, the old sixteenth-century timber-framed Market/Council House in North Street and the Guildhall in the Priory. The old Market House in the carriageway of North Street had an open ground floor for the market traders and stairs leading to the Council Chamber on the first floor.

The mayor and council also used the Swan Inn for occasional meetings at this time, as well as the Market House and members' homes. These draughty and old buildings were causing problems for the council.

With the support of Charles Lennox, second Duke of Richmond, plans for the erection of a new building were prepared. On the 28 November 1728, the council agreed to pull down the old Market House and build a New Town Hall. The council then bought land from John Miller for two hundred and eighty pounds for the new building.

After the move to the new Council House in North Street in 1730 – 1731, they arranged to demolish the old building.

Council House, North Street, Chichester, West Sussex PO19 1LQ

On the 9 March 1730, the Corporation gave four hundred pounds for the construction work and the balance of the cash was to come from public subscription. However, there was a shortfall of funds, as only £1189 1s 0d was raised. The largest contributor was the Duke of Richmond. He had presented the council with £363 10s 0d and total funds were then achieved.

Between 1731 and 1733, the new baroque style Council House, built on land acquired from Sir John Miller, was erected in the centre of North Street. The London architect, Roger Morris, designed the building.

The total costs including land were £1271 15s 11d and the old wooden Market and Council House was demolished.

The first recorded meeting of the council in their new home was on the 11 August 1732.

The new rectangular building is in red brick, Portland stone with five bays, and tiled roof with arches on columns and facing North Street.

On the first floor, there are four more stone columns and at the top of the façade inscribed in Latin:

"In order that the Council and the people of Chichester and their posterity might be happy and fortunate, this Council House was begun and completed in the year of our Lord 1731, in the reign of George II, elector and king."

The Council Chamber built in 1731, is at the front of the building, with a deeply coved ceiling and an eighteenth-century chandelier. At either end of the room are decorated wooden fireplaces with pediment over the mantels. There were panels on the side where they could display portraits. The names of former mayors since 1532 are displayed on boards hanging on the wall. There is also the Mayor's Parlour, added in 1880 – 1881, when the Old Courtroom was built. This was now home for the Corporation and the Common Council that later became the Chichester City Council.

In 1781 - 1783, the council arranged for a new East Wing designed by James Wyatt and erected in plain brick by Thomas Andrews, a local builder. The costs of the works were fourteen hundred pounds. The Corporation paid two hundred pounds and the balance came from public subscription.

Later, due to a shortfall of funds, the Corporation elected to contribute a further fifty pounds. This became the Assembly Rooms with a new anteroom connecting to the Council House and officially opened on the 11 October 1783.

The main room is sixty feet long, thirty-eight feet wide and a height of twenty-four feet. There was a music gallery on the south wall between large fireplaces. This room could seat three hundred and twenty people.

There were further expansions made and repairs to the building in 1881 with the construction of a new Courthouse, both built by public subscription. They had been holding courts in the Council Chamber, which was proving very challenging. The recorder, J. J. Johnson, opened the new Courthouse in April 1881. On the 5 July 1950, the Council House became a listed Grade II building.

There were more plans for changes approved in 1970, and there were major restoration works carried out in 1976 by John Fowler. Some years later, in 1992, there was further refurbishment. Later in 2002, The Hunt Partnership of Southsea carried out major repairs and in May 2002, the tenth Earl of Richmond officiated at the reopening.

By the new changes after the Local Government Act 1974, Chichester District Council came into being. It was formed from the amalgamation of the Rural Districts of Midhurst, Petworth and part of the Chichester Rural District. With the City of Chichester and the towns of Midhurst, Petworth and Selsey there are sixty-eight civil parishes within the council's authority.

In the past, the Westhampnett Rural District Council (1895 – 1933), of which Selsey was part of, held meetings in the workhouse in Westhampnett, until a fire destroyed the building on the 3 November 1899. They moved to offices in East Street, Chichester before moving again to 5, South Street where they were from 1907 until 1918. Finally, they bought and moved to Pallant House in 1919 where they stayed until their last meeting on 31 March 1933

Pallant House, a refined 1712 house, built by Henry Smart for Henry 'Lisbon' Peckham, a local wine merchant and his wife Elizabeth. It is a fine two-storey building in red brick with brick quoins. Set back from the pavement it has seven window bays and the roof with attic windows. There is a grand entrance with Corinthian pilasters.

On the 5 July 1950, the building received a Grade I listing.

Pallant House
9, North Pallant, Chichester, West Sussex. PO19 1TJ

On the 1 April 1933 saw the creation of the new Chichester Rural District Council and they elected Arthur C. Harris JP their chairman. He had been the chair of the now-replaced Westhampnett Council. They took over the responsibilities of the Westhampnett Rural District Council with their first meeting on 7 April and stayed in the building until 1979.

After the council moved out restoration work began on the building in 1979 and the Pallant House Gallery opened in 1982. Since 1985, an independent trust has been in charge of the management. The gallery is world renowned for holding the finest collections of twentieth-century British art. In June 2006, a new £8.6m modern wing opened which the Arts Council England, Heritage Lottery Fund, local council and other private donors funded. The new wing designed by Long & Kentish architects, in association with Sir Colin Alexander St John Wilson, the architect of the British Library.

Chichester District Council, East Pallant House, 1, East Pallant, Chichester, West Sussex PO19 1TY

Chichester Rural District Council was formed on 1 April 1933 and took up offices in Pallant House. Later they moved to East Pallant House in 1979. With the reorganisations of the Local Government Act 1972, the council became the Chichester District Council on 1 April 1974. R.S. Hancock became their first chairman.

This two storeys Georgian building of 1745, owned by Robert Bull (a former JP and mayor), has had many changes over the years including a new Council Chamber. There are large double bow-fronted windows on each side of the door that has a pediment with Doric columns. Since the 5 July 1950, the building has received a Grade II listing.

After constructing a new extension, HNW local architects with Pope Building Services installed forty solar panels on a refurbished roof of the building.

The District Council still occupies this building with its main entrance in the new extension.

West Sussex County Council

After the Local Government Act 1888, West Sussex County Council set up in 1889 from the Rapes of Chichester, Arundel and Bramber inherited control over this area of the county. For a short period, this council overlapped the old council. In January 1889, R.B. Willis was appointed chairman until the first full business meeting in the Council House, North Street on 4 April 1889. Charles Gordon-Lennox, the sixth Duke of Richmond and Gordon, became chairman and held the post until the 1903 elections. Later the council met in Horsham, Petworth and Chichester and like Lewes in East Sussex the councils carried on business in many different buildings.

Eighteen fifty-seven saw the forming of the West Sussex Constabulary and they had their headquarters in Petworth until the 1880s when they moved into new offices.

In 1913, the council were using offices all over the county. The clerk had offices in shop buildings in Horsham; the County Surveyor used a room in his house, as did the County Medical Officer in Worthing. Also, in Worthing were the Education and Health departments and the County Treasurer occupied rooms in a house in West Street, Chichester. This was proving inefficient and extremely difficult to carry on council business. So West Sussex County Council in 1922 moved from the Town Hall in Horsham to John Edes House in West Street Chichester. Then later in 1936, they moved into the new purpose-built County Hall.

With the birth of the NHS in July 1948, county councils had a statutory obligation to provide an ambulance service. In West Sussex, the council hired St John's Ambulance Brigade to supply the service and refunded them for their expenses. The exception was in Midhurst where the Red Cross supplied this service. It was not until 1966 that the council had direct control and managed the service.

There were major transformations in the 1973 reforms with boundary changes in the East of the county. This caused the breakup of the Urban Councils of Burgess Hill, Cuckfield and East Grinstead. They then became absorbed into the new West Sussex County Council under the Mid Sussex District Council administration.

The first meeting of the new council on the 27 April 1973 elected Sir Peter Mursell as their chairman.

The County Council now has offices in County Hall Chichester as well as County Hall, North Horsham. This was the former Royal and Sun Alliance 1994 building known as Parkside in Horsham where the council held their first meeting on the 21 October 2009. The total cost of the building and refurbishment costs were about £20m. Further local offices are at Centenary House in Worthing (1988 - 1989), Durban House in Bognor Regis (2006) and in the Crawley Library building in Crawley.

Within the authority of the County Council, there are seven district and borough councils. In addition, there are one hundred and fifty-nine town, parish and neighbourhood councils.

John Edes House, West Street, Chichester, West Sussex. PO19 1QW

In 1916, the County Council bought John Edes house built in 1696 for John Edes a local maltster. The price paid was five thousand five hundred pounds and it became the County Hall.

Because of the upheaval of World War 1, the council did not move from Horsham into the building until 1922. They occupied John Edes House until 1936 and the completion of the present new County Hall.

The building is red brick and Portland stone with two storeys, seven bays, attic and basement. There are two slightly projecting wings with a dormer in each topped with a tiled hipped roof and lead ridges. There is a pediment over the central portion of the building. The building since the 5 July 1950 has a Grade I listing.

In modern times, there have been some changes to the front of the building and the floors strengthened in 1967 – 1968 to house the West Sussex Records office. For a short period they occupied the building. The county council still use the house for meetings and other artistic and ceremonial activities.

County Hall, West Street, Chichester, West Sussex PO19 1RQ

In 1933 – 1936, construction for a new County Hall building began in the large orchard of John Edes House. C.G. Stillman the county architect designed this with support from Stanley Roth. The new hall is a large concrete and brick-clad building. In Neo-Georgian style with eleven bays in the centre, a large central doorway and projecting wings both left and right. The tiles were handmade and the bricks came from Rickmansworth, with windows and joinery made in Dover. The building costs were one hundred thousand pounds and the building officially opened in April 1936. During World War 2, the County's control centre was under the Council Chamber in County Hall.

The 1960s saw the construction of the West Sussex County Emergency Centre in the basement of County Hall. In the 'L' shaped control room, there was a large table with maps leading to telephone rooms. As well as a small dormitory and generator room with access from a flight of stairs behind the main reception desk.

In early 2014 asbestos was discovered in the ceiling of the council chamber. July saw work started on removing the roof, ceiling, and disposing of the asbestos.

Crawley

This is an old town tracing its history back to the Stone (Neolithic) Age with slow early development compared to its neighbours of Horsham and East Grinstead. There were Iron Age forts created for the extraction of iron ore from the surrounding area and the Romans later expanded these. The first record of the town holding a market licence was in 1203 when these extended around the church. The parish was in the Rape of Lewes and the Hundred of Buttinghill. The town's name from the Anglo-Saxon 'Crawe Leah' has changed overtime and the spelling we now have is from about 1316.

Although, on a major road between London and Brighton and being a mail stopover, there was no District Council formed until the Crawley Urban District Council of May 1956. Before this local control was in the hands of Horsham Rural District Council (in West Sussex), Cuckfield Rural District Council (East Sussex) and Dorking and Horley Rural District Council (Surrey).

By 1956 the population of the new town had grown to thirty thousand and R. May was elected as the chairman of the council. In 1973 - 1974, Jim G. Smith was the last chairman of the District Council serving from July 1973 until March 1974. Later in April 1974 and after the Local Government Act 1972 they changed to the Crawley Borough Council. This was the first time the town had a mayoral office. Jim G. Smith filled the post from April 1974 until May when Cllr B. Clay held the position. In the years 1976 – 1977, 1996 – 1997 and 2004 - 2005 Mr Smith was re-elected to serve the town.

After the arrival of the railway in the 1840s the town started to expand. The first rail station was at Three Bridges in 1841 and known as East Crawley. Later in 1848, a new station opened at the South end of the High Street.

The Crawley Volunteer Fire Brigade was formed in 1866 with its fire station in Ifield Road. One of its main patrons was Mark Lemon a Crawley resident, co-founder of 'Punch' magazine and friend of Charles Dickens.

Expansion continued with the racecourse in 1891 and later in the late 1920s Gatwick Aerodrome. The airfield first obtained commercial flight licences in 1933. After new owners and renovations, Lord Swinton, the Secretary of State, on the 6 June 1936 opened the new airport. During the war the RAF requisitioned the airfield in 1939. Then later in June 1958, after a £7.8m redevelopment, was reopened by HM The Queen as Gatwick Airport.

After the Second World War, and the 1946 New Towns Act there was much discussion in Parliament about forming New Towns in England.

The government selected eight towns around London for expansion and in February 1947, the Crawley Development Corporation came into being. The chairman was Thomas Bennett an architect and the Corporation housed at Broadfield House, an 1830 villa set in extensive parkland.

Broadfield House, Crawley, West Sussex. RH11 9RZ

In late 1947 the Corporation bought the villa, refitted it and by 23 August 1948, it opened as their headquarters. In mid-1949 James Longley & Co, local builders erected extra buildings in the grounds to house the architects and engineers offices.

The building on the Tilgate Estate in Broadfield Park is on the South of the town. This is a fine villa style house on two storeys with a low Welsh slate roof and an internal design in the Greek revival style. It has deep projecting eaves and its main entrance is situated on the north side. There are five windows facing east from the front and a columned veranda facing the lake. Added to the building in 1860 was the large hall with three bays, round-arched windows and a first-floor gallery.

The first owner of the house was Rev William Serigson and ownership has passed through many hands until the early 1940s.

The London Carriage Company converted the building into a hotel and country club until the New Towns Commission took possession. It then became the headquarters of the Crawley Development Corporation.

Broadfield House has since the 21 June 1948 been a Grade II listed building.

Between May 1960 and March 1962, the Council held their meetings in The Hall, West Green County Junior School in West Green Drive.

Under the terms of the New Towns Act, the Crawley Development Corporation would end when a new town was substantially complete. By 1962 with a population now at sixty thousand the Crawley Development Corporation passed all assets over to the Commission for New Towns. Later in 1978, the Corporation handed over the commission's assets to the recently formed borough.

Today Crawley is the largest inland town in West Sussex and was the last town in the county of Sussex to get incorporation, which it did in 1974.

For some years, Broadfield House was empty until the local radio station Radio Mercury acquired the building in 1984. Later in 2011, there was £1.9m refurbishment of the building. This was then taken over by the free school known as the Discovery New School, which closed after losing it's funding in April 2014.

The Boulevard, Crawley, West Sussex, RH10 1UZ

After the original plans presented were rejected as being too expensive, in 1961, the Council accepted a plan for a New Town Hall.

In 1963, the architects Sir John Brown & Henson and builders Humphreys Ltd built the Town Hall that incorporated the Police station and Courts.

The Rt. Hon Michael Stewart MP, Secretary of State for Education and Science, officially opened the New Town Hall on the 14 November 1964. The total building costs came to four hundred and forty-eight thousand two hundred pounds. The costs were the land at ten thousand two hundred pounds, building three hundred and sixty thousand pounds, fees at fifty-three thousand pounds and furniture and fittings of twenty-five thousand pounds. The building in concrete and glass is in typical 1960s style and stands five storeys high.

There was an extension built in 1979 and in the cellars of the Town Hall in 1989, a nuclear bunker and shelter was built. Its main aim was to be a command centre in case of an emergency but nowadays used for storage. Just as well as the escape hatch outside the Town Hall, and now in the car park is blocked. There were dormitories, toilets, kitchen, controller's room and a rest room.

In 2007, there was a discussion about building a New Town Hall but, after the 2009 financial crisis, all plans are on hold. In 2013, the Council, in an attempt to save electricity costs, installed one hundred and ninety-four solar panels on the roof above the Council Chamber costing £74,514.

Haywards Heath

The first mention of the village is in deeds of 1265 when the name used was 'Heyworthe'. Haywards Heath was a small hamlet with two inns, nine cottages, farms and a windmill and only started to grow when the railway arrived on 12 July 1841. This was extended to Brighton on 21 September. It became a town in 1862. There was a sizeable market in 1859 that by 1900 had become the county's largest cattle market.

Boltro Road for many years has been the hub of local governance in Haywards Heath with different buildings used by various councils. From the Victorian Villas to twentieth-century brick buildings and private houses occupied by solicitors and the town clerks. Sadly, most of these buildings over the years have gone because of modernization of the town.

The Local Board set up in 1872 when Haywards Heath was part of the old civil parish of Cuckfield and continued until the reforms of 1894.

The first chairman of the board was Richard Pannett, a local landowner and builder. Meetings were at the surveyor's office in Perrymount Road, or the Station Hotel in Market Place and later in offices on Boltro Road. After 1894, when the town became a district parish, governance passed to the Haywards Heath Urban District Council (1894 - 1934) and their first chairman was Thomas Bannister a local auctioneer.

Originally, the council, created with nine members, held meetings in Boltro Road between the years of 1894 and 1934.

In 1901, the Cuckfield Rural District Council arranged for Arthur Richard Pannett, a local architect, to design a new red brick and Bath stone council office further along in Boltro Road. The builder appointed was Stephen King of Cuckfield. On the first floor, there was a spacious Council Chamber with two further Committee rooms and more offices on the floor above.

A feature of the new offices was a large stained-glass window at the top of the main staircase. The window integrated a representation of the authority's seal with its centrepiece a view of the arched gateway to Cuckfield Park. The cost of the building was about six thousand five hundred pounds. Major J Lister JP chairman of the Rural Council laid the foundation stone for the new building on the 22 November 1901. They met here until the reforms of 1974 and the building was later demolished in 1987 and replaced by general offices.

In 1903, the Urban District Council erected a council building in South Road for the surveyor's department (1903 – 1934). It contained meeting rooms, and on the ground floor, public conveniences and the Fire Station.

Haywards Heath Volunteer Fire Brigade was formed originally in 1889 with just a hose cart and fire hose. From about 1894, their home was in The Yews on the corner of Boltro Road and Munster Green. Later in 1903, they moved to South Road.

The council moved out, but the Fire Station was in use until 1961 and their move to Mill Green Road. In 1981, the council decided to demolish the building.

After the Local Government Act 1929, and the East Sussex County Council's review, Haywards Heath and Cuckfield Urban District councils merged in April 1934.

They formed the new Cuckfield Urban District Council (1934 – April 1974) and the last chairman of Haywards Heath Urban District Council was William Sandford Poole. The first chairman of the new council was Charles Hales, a JP and a director of the Tate and Lyle Company.

Meetings were held at the Queens Hall in Cuckfield. A large Victorian hall erected in 1897, with a Council Chamber, and used up to 1933. The council then moved offices to Oaklands in Haywards Heath. The last chairman of the Cuckfield Urban District Council was R.J. Woolacott (1973-1974).

With the reforms of 1974, Haywards Heath and Burgess Hill transferred and came under West Sussex county administration.

40 Boltro Road, Haywards Heath, West Sussex, RH16 1BA

Later, following the reforms, the Haywards Heath Town Council came into being and succeeded the Neighbourhood Council, which had been set up two years earlier. W.W. Chick in 1987 was the first mayor of Haywards Heath. Cuckfield reverted to Parish Council status in April 1986 and still meets at the Queen's Hall in the High Street.

The Haywards Heath Neighbourhood Council met in rooms in Sydney Street until in October and the move by the Town Council to the New Town Hall.

A & J Mighell, builders of Steyning, built the Georgian style Town Hall with a portico and balcony. The costs were two hundred and seventy thousand pounds. The council chamber was on the ground floor at the back of the building. Chairman Cllr David Brazell officially opened the building on the 12 October 1990.

Mid-Sussex District Council

Oaklands, Oaklands Road, Haywards Heath,
West Sussex. RH16 1SS

With the reforms and boundary changes in 1974, the Urban Councils of Burgess Hill, Cuckfield, and East Grinstead and the Rural District Council of Cuckfield transferred to West Sussex County Council. Mid Sussex District Council now governs them.

There are twenty-four Parish and Town Councils under this title and Mid Sussex District Council have their offices in Oaklands, in Oaklands Road alongside Boltro Road.

They had originally moved into offices in the old Cuckfield Rural District Council's property in Boltro Road before the building was taken down. The new council also had offices in Albion House, Boltro Road, a large Victorian house that was demolished in 1987.

The first chairperson of the newly formed Mid-Sussex District Council was Margaret Lister Williams, who was also the last chairperson of the now defunct Cuckfield Rural District Council.

Oaklands was built on land bought from the Sergison family in 1864 for over three hundred pounds by Mr Treacher from Brighton. He was a former chairman of the Local Board. The building was sold in 1892 to James Bradford and later in 1932, to his daughter Mrs Burgoyne.

The Cuckfield Urban District Council in 1933 purchased Oaklands at a cost five thousand one hundred pounds. In 1975 and again in 1985 there were extra modern offices added to the building.

Horsham

This is an old market town. In the Rape of Bramber and Hundred of Singlecross whose history dates from the Saxon times. Its name came from hors-ham – the horses' meadow. The town is known to have been a Parliamentary Borough since 1295. Horsham expanded well over the years until the reforms of 1885. After the Lighting and Watching Act 1833, a board of inspectors was set up and one of their duties was to manage the town fire engine.

A Local Board founded in July 1875 with Robert Henry Hurst MP as chairman, governed the town until 1894. The Board had offices in London Road (1882 – 1887) and then moved into the Town Hall (1887 – 1894).

In December 1894, the town Board became the Urban District Council (1894 – 1974) after the new government act of that year. Then they held their first elections. Since 1974 the District Council has governed the town, and West Sussex County Council has large offices in the town.

The Horsham District Council was made up with the merger of both the Horsham Rural and Urban District Councils and Chanctonbury Rural District Council formed on 1 April 1974. The new chairman was David Ives Bosaquet. Although having an ancient Town Hall, the council have offices in many different buildings in Horsham.

Now they have decided to share the building, County Hall North, with the West Sussex County Council to cut the costs of running the local administration.

Market Square in the centre of town was the site of the original Town Hall - Market House with an open arcade for stallholders. The upper floor used for public business.

Lord Charles Eversfield MP and Arthur Ingram, the sixth Viscount of Irvine rebuilt the building in 1721. The new building had a two-storey hipped slate roof with three-bay entrance façade on the front facing north and five-bayed façade on the east and west in Portland stone. There was an open ground floor used as a market and the first floor used for town business with a large council room. Later because of the building becoming unstable rebuilding was necessary again.

1 Market Square, Horsham, West Sussex RH12 1EU

Thanks to a gift from Henry Charles Howard, thirteenth Duke of Norfolk, in 1812, there were repairs to the building. At the same time, they enlarged the building using local stone. With a new façade, which had a coat of arms of Coade stone and was built in the Norman style. The cost was eight thousand pounds.

At the south end beneath the new stone stairway, was a recess where they stored the town's fire engine.

The ground floor was enclosed and used as a lower courtroom and in the basement were three timber cells, two for men and one for women.

The cells in the basement were in use up to the time of the new police station in Queens Street in 1846. In 1820, the Duke of Norfolk gifted a clock to the town, which was made by W.H. Bailey of Manchester. On either side of the clock tower, there are three bells. Two from 1889 and cast in Croydon and one with the date 1820. By 1830, the building was again in disrepair and dangerous and the Spring Assizes moved to Lewes.

Under the control of the Urban Council, in 1840, they created the new Horsham Volunteer Fire Brigade. Earlier before 1724, a fire engine had been gifted to the parish. Later Lady Irwin presented a fire engine to the town in 1780. The brigade stored their escape ladders at the Town Hall until 1883 when they moved to North Street. This new building bought for four hundred and eighty-five pounds with two hundred pounds raised by local subscription also housed two fire engines. These had previously been at the engine house in the northwest corner of Carfax.

There was a public meeting held in March 1867 to decide the fate of the Town Hall. After much discussion, there was an agreement to accept an offer from the Duke for a ninety-year lease at an annual cost of one pound. Local ratepayers, who undertook to look after the building, chose three trustees. They were Robert Henry Hurst, John Aldridge and William Lintott, an MP, a soldier (Major) and a local merchant. Two years later the town raised money by public subscription for repairs and a mortgage of £288 15s 0d from the Horsham Building Society (20 November 1869). The Local Board took over the lease with £207 12s 1d outstanding on the 24 March 1876. Later, on the 28 May 1888, the Duke of Norfolk signed the conveyance of the Town Hall over to the Local Board.

It was necessary for repair works on the building in 1869 but by 1888, more problems had emerged again. Because of restricted funds, there were repairs to the structure rather than replace the building.

The fifteenth Duke sold the building freehold to the town for twenty-five pounds in 1888. The Local Board arranged in the autumn of 1888 for J. Percy Gates, architect and surveyor of Dolphin Chambers, New Shoreham to undertake the work. Local builder Joseph Potter assisted him. The price for works was one thousand five hundred pounds.

There were extensive repairs made to the west wall and the clock moved from the tower to a central position on the front Norman façade of the Town Hall. By 1889, the works were complete.

There were two large halls of forty-three feet by thirty-one feet each. A committee room some twenty-five feet by seventeen feet six inches, and various offices. The Council Chamber had the capacity to hold three hundred people for council or social meetings.

The Urban District Council (1894 – 1974) first met on 31 December 1894 and elected Capt. Norman A. MacCleod as the first chairman of the council. They held their regular meetings in the Town Hall until the reforms of 1974. The Quarter Sessions held their meetings also in the Town Hall until 1939. The Law Courts were operating until 1974.

The council also used additional offices at 14 Market Square and Park House in Horsham Park.

For a time, West Sussex County Council held their meetings in the Town Hall, as Horsham was joint county town with Chichester. These meetings were from 1888 until 1915 - 1916 when Chichester became the sole county town.

Around 1958, the clock was becoming unreliable and by 1976, the council considered its replacement. They then assigned funds for the repairs.

Source: *"West Sussex County Times, September 24, 1976. Some months later, the clock came back to life again when local watchmaker Terry Callaghan wound the mechanism up. He estimated that another £40 - 50 would be needed to correct the problems with the mechanism".*

The Town Hall, which, since the 23 October 2009, has had a Grade II listing, no longer handles council business. The Horsham Registry Office moved into the building until 2009 and their following move to Park House.

In 2004, there were major repairs and refurbishments to the Town Hall costing two hundred thousand pounds.

The council finally left the building in 2009 and put a lease out to tender for a commercial company to look after this listed building.

Again, in 2012, Crickmay Chartered Surveyors of Horsham and Davis Coffer Lyons of London put the Town Hall up for sale at the price of £1m. Alternatively, they offered a lease for sixty-five thousand pounds a year.

For the time being, this is the end of the civic use of the old Town Hall. Since October 2012, the council has granted a lease to a commercial company and the ground floor is now a popular restaurant.

Comewell House, North Street,
Horsham, West Sussex RH12 1RD

After the Local Government Act 1894, the newly formed Horsham Rural District Council (1894 – 1973) held their first meeting on 1 May 1895. Their elected chairman was Robert Hurst. They held their monthly meetings at the Town Hall until 1934.

They were also using offices in Carfax and at 42, Albion Terrace for day-to-day business.

In October 1935, the council decided to build new offices and in 1936 - 1937, they commissioned work to start on Comewell House, North Street. The architects chosen were Good and Kay.

The costs of the building were twelve hundred pounds for the site, six thousand five hundred pounds for the building and eight hundred and fifty-five pounds for miscellaneous expenses.

They stayed in North Street until the council was wound up in 1973. Group Force Security and DHL have since used the building as well as other smaller businesses

Park House, Horsham Park, Horsham, West Sussex. RH12 1RN

A former Town Hall, this early eighteenth-century provincial house now named Park House (1930), was built in red brick, two storeys with central pediment and attic with Horsham stone roof.

With nine bays of windows to the front and facing the park at the rear, it has seven bays with Portland stone architraves to each window. The building was formerly a private home known as Horsham Park. The house stands in grounds of a former dwelling of John Michell who died in 1522. By 1701, ownership had passed to the John Wicker's family. Situated on the Southern edge of Horsham Park, John Wicker, later to be Lord Nutham, rebuilt the house sometime between 1690 and 1720.

There were further changes of ownership until in 1799 Robert Hurst MP bought the building and grounds from the Smith family and owned the house until 1928.

It was Col A.R. Hurst who sold the house and grounds in 1928 to the Urban District Council for eighteen thousand pounds. Later Park House became a listed Grade II building on the 20 May 1949.

Horsham Urban District Council used the house (1930-1974) until they sold it to Horsham District Council.

Later, major repairs were needed because of a fire that started in the library in 1979. As this was an important historic building, James Longley & Co Ltd of Crawley started work on the 11 January 1982 on restoring the building. Meanwhile, the council used various offices in the town.

Horsham District Council still uses the house for administrative offices. In 2009, the Horsham Registry Office moved into the ground floor to conduct weddings and civil partnerships.

In 2014, the District Council put the building up for sale as part of the council's reorganisation plans. An update to these plans in 2015 and the council on advice from their estate agents have decided to offer unused offices on short leases. For now, the building freehold will remain in council hands.

New Park House, North Street, Horsham,
West Sussex. RH12 1RJ

As the council was in need of extra offices, James Longley & Co Ltd of Crawley won a contract of £1.1m to erect a new red brick building for the expanding needs of the council. The contract finished ahead of schedule.

When completed the chairman of the District Council, David Keen officially opened New Park House in December 1982.

This building was in use by the council until the early 2000s when Horsham Primary Care Trust moved into the building.

Park North, North Street, Horsham, West Sussex RH12 1RL

Built in 1987 - 1988, the new red brick offices were officially opened on the 16 March 1988 by the chairman of the District Council, Cllr John Burningham MBE. Park North is still the home of the District Council that came into being on the 1 April 1974 with the merger of the Horsham and Chanctonbury Rural District Councils.

The town does not have a mayor but forty-four District Councillors. Each May they elect a new chairman to represent the council for civic and ceremonial purposes. Within the district, there are thirty-two parishes including Steyning and the Horsham district.

This building was the home of the Horsham District Council Emergency Centre built in the basement, with the help of a grant of eighty per cent from the Home Office. There were dormitories and a ventilation plant room, with a blast door leading to a small filter room that purified air through micron filters. Opposite this was the control room with a door leading to a further four rooms and a small kitchen with enough food, fuel and water for twenty-five people for at least a fortnight.

To save the local council costs in November 2013 there was a plan to move into County Hall North and share the building with the County Council. The building would be renamed Parkside (May 2015). The councils reached an agreement and the District Council moved into the building and held their first council meeting on 20 May 2015. Park North will be put up for sale.

County Hall North, Chart Way, Horsham, West Sussex. RH12 1XH

West Sussex

With the forming of the West Sussex County Council in 1888, they met regularly in the Town Hall in Horsham as well as in Petworth and Chichester. The County Council also had offices at 51, East Street between 1914 and 1923.

In 2008, the County Council bought Parkside, a 1993 building which was the former Royal and Sun Alliance building. They then converted it into the new West Sussex County Councils offices in Horsham. The costs were about £7.2m and the building renamed as County Hall North. The council did not meet all the costs, as there were grants central government were offering. The architects and surveyors for the project were Brodie Plant Goddard of Dorking, Surrey with Wates Group Limited of Leatherhead, Surrey. The builders also made a new entrance canopy and refurbished all mechanical and electrical equipment. During the time of reconstruction, the staff moved in on a phased occupation. The Cabinet held their first full meeting on the 20 October 2009.

In 2014, the Horsham District Council was in negotiations to share the building with the West Sussex County Council. After a mutual agreement the Horsham District Council made their move on 20 May 2015.

Midhurst

The Old Town Hall, Market Square, Midhurst, West Sussex, GU29 9NJ

The town's name comes from the Saxon, 'midden' and 'hirst' a place in the midst of woody ground. A borough by prescription it was in the Rape of Chichester, the Hundred of Easebourne, and a thriving market town. Midhurst was a 'free borough' until it lost its borough status in 1886 after the Municipal Corporation Act 1882. A Bailiff governed the town and the last Bailiff of Midhurst was William H Packham.

The Rural Sanitary Authority created in 1872 to manage the town's affairs, became the Rural District Council when it formed in January 1895 (1895 - 1974). They were meeting at the Midhurst Union Workhouse in Easebourne until 1899, with Col H.A. Lascelles as their chairman. The new council used offices in town until 1903 - 1938 when they met at the Town Hall in Market Square, Midhurst.

By 1939 until 1974 they had moved their meetings to the Council Offices in North Street that were later taken over by the new Chichester District Council.

On the 20 October 1552, Sir Anthony Browne the Lord of the Manor of Cowdray gave land, a vacant plot seventy feet by thirty feet, to the town's burgesses. They then built the old Market House/Hall. This is the building that Gilbert Hanham started his Grammar School in the upper loft in 1672. They rebuilt and converted the old hall into the 'Town Hall' in 1760.

The two storeys Town Hall was built on the south side of Market Square. It has a hipped slate roof, ground floor rusticates and the west front is stuccoed. On the north side, there is now an outside staircase leading to the first floor, the sidewalls are filled with stone rubble. It was a building originally with an open ground floor but now with modern windows. In about 1843, William Mercer & Son, builders from Knockhundred Row, renovated the Town Hall, and the roof renewed, as the upper part was unsafe, probably with the patronage of the Smith family. During the renovations, they removed the stairs from the interior of the building.

The Magistrates, who used to sit at The Angel Hotel, in April 1848 moved to the upper floors, where they stayed until moving to their new property in Grange Road. There were cells in the lower part of the building and the parish stocks used to be outside the west end of the building.

Midhurst has had two railway stations. The London and South Western Railway opened the first in September 1864 on the Petersfield line. This service closed in 1925. The London Brighton and South Coast Railway opened another station in October 1866. This was on the Pulborough - Petworth line and continued to carry passengers until February 1955 and freight until October 1964.

The Parish fire engine was kept in a store place behind the original building, and from here in 1793 travelled to the devastating fire in Cowdray House on the 24 September.

With the establishment in 1865 of the Voluntary Fire Brigade, they stationed their two-horse drawn appliances at the back of the Town Hall and their horses held in fields close by at St. Annes. Later the fire brigade took over the complete building until they left in 1955 for a new fire station at the Wharf.

When the Rural District Council bought a Delaunay-Belleville motor fire engine there had to be changes at the front of the building to house the engine. They widened the doorway and lowered the floor by two feet to facilitate the new appliance.

In 1934, the brigade replaced the fire engine with an English Leyland Cub appliance. On the building were two fire bells, which are still there today. The building since 26 November 1987 has a Grade II listing.

By an arrangement of the Charity Commissioners, on the 4 February 1910, the Midhurst Town Trust took over the administration of the Town Hall, Market Square and the Pound, Bepton Road. The Town Trust now owns the freehold of the Town Hall and the ground floor is leased out for commercial use.

Although becoming Rural District Council, the town lost that status in 1974 with the 1972 reforms and became a Town Council with E.W. Knight elected as the first chairman. The town has chosen not to elect anyone to the office of mayor and has regularly elected a chairperson to lead the council. They held meetings in North Street offices until their move to Capron House in 1986.

Three authorities, namely the Midhurst Town Council, Chichester District Council and West Sussex County Council now govern the town.

Chichester District Council Offices and Midhurst Town Council are now in a part of Capron House (1986- 2014), North Street, Midhurst, West Sussex, GU29 9DS. The Cowdray estate owns the building.

Petworth

Market Square, Petworth, West Sussex. GU28 0AJ

The town Petworth is a market town and was in the Hundred of Rotherbridge and Rape of Arundel. Mentioned in the Domesday Book of 1086 as 'Peteorde' and known now mainly for the stately home of Petworth House and its fine gardens landscaped by L. Capability Brown in the late 1750s. In the past, there were ironworks and glass was also made in the town. On the 20 November each year they hold a fair in the town and this is a tradition carried forward from ancient times.

From October 1859 until February 1955, the town had its own railway station, although this was almost two miles outside the town. The line, part of the Pulborough to Midhurst service, carried freight until May 1966. The station building is now a guesthouse.

This former Town Hall was a private house. In 1793, the third Earl of Egremont (1751–1837) built the house on the site of a former medieval timber Market House. It is a two-storey building of local sandstone with slate roof and housed the court on the first floor. Mounted on the roof at the front of the building the town's three fire bells with a bust of William III in an oval niche in the North wall.

In 1869, there was work to extend the building westwards and then again further improvements in 1891.

There were prisoner cells installed, one on the ground floor and one below ground level.

In addition, there was another cell in the roof space above the Hall entrance.

Petworth Fire Brigade in 1895 had a fire engine and hose stationed in the Town Hall until 1920 when the council bought a Model T Ford fire engine. They moved out in 1935 to a building next to the town's mortuary.

The Town Hall was in use until the 1950s when its formal municipal use ended. Since the 22 February 1955, the Town Hall building has a Grade II listing

In 1959, after alterations to the hall, its owner John Wyndham, later to become Lord Egremont, gave it to the town. The buildings management is now in the hands of the Leconfield Hall Trust, a registered charity.

In 1992 and again in 1998 there were major restoration works undertaken on both the interior and outside of the hall. After raising funds from a large legacy from a local resident, with grants from the English Heritage, the National Lottery and others this helped pay the costs. There is a board inside the hall with the names of all the contributors.

The Leconfield Estate undertook these works after winning the contract with the best tender in a competition. With the discovery of the three original fire bells in the basement, the Trust restored them to their previous position on the front of the building. Extra funding from West Sussex County Council made it possible to install a new clock.

Petworth Rural District Council (1895 – 1974) was the local government from January 1895 after the Local Government Act 1894 and succeeded the Rural Sanitary Authority, formed in 1872. The first chairman elected at the meeting on the 14 December 1894 was the solicitor, Arthur French Mant. The council held meetings at either the Town Hall or the Institute. In the 1950s, the council services moved offices to the corner of Station Road, Midhurst Road and Pound Street.

The early ambulance service also used these offices. The Poor Law Institute, Wisborough Green built in 1820 was occasionally used for meetings.

After the reforms of 1974, the Petworth Parish Council took over governance of the town with Bert Speed elected their first chairman.

In May 2009 at the Parish Council Meeting the chairman, Andrew Howard, announced the name of the council would change to Town Council.

Ken Lintill became the newly elected chairman. The new council declined the opportunity to elect a mayor into office. Elections for the Town Council are held every four years.

The Chichester District Council used to have an area office at Newlands in Pound Street, where the parish council offices were, but moved in the late 1990s to Golden Square and has since left the town.

The town now comes under the governance of the small Petworth Town Council, created in May 2009, Chichester District Council (1974) and the West Sussex County Council.

Mrs Jean D. Huggett, a former chair of Petworth Parish Council, was the Clerk until recently when Mrs Rebecca Knifton took on the duties for Petworth Town Council. Their offices are at The Old Bakery, Golden Square, Petworth, West Sussex, GU28 0AP a former home of the Chichester District Council.

Portslade

Victoria Road, Portslade, West Sussex BN41 1YF

The small town of Portslade originally in the Rape of Lewes and the Hundred of Fishergate was governed by the Portslade Urban District Council, which came into being on the 1 April 1898. Previously the town was part of the Steyning East Rural District Council.

Originally, the village of Portslade inland from the coast changed when the railway arrived in 1840. This brought about the development of the coastal area known as Copperas Gap at the southern end of the village and renamed as Portslade on Sea. The old village is proud of its history and its own identity. In 1909, a fire station was built in Church Road. It was constructed of white glazed brick with terracotta dressings and had a hipped roof and was in use until 1946.

Council meetings took place in Station Road until 1903 and then at St. Andrews National School. Later they moved to the Council Assembly Rooms, Church Road in 1911 where they stayed until 1915. From 1915 until 1960, they were at 17 Station Road. Charles Rose was their first elected chairman with twelve members forming the council.

The Urban District Council in 1959 bought the old reception hall used by the Ronuk Polish factory for thirty-six thousand five hundred pounds.

Robert Shields, chairman of the UDC officially opened the new building and they named it the Portslade Town Hall.

This hall originally built in 1927 and known as the Ronuk Hall and Welfare Institute was for recreation use of the company's employees for many years.

Gilbert M Simpson designed the red brick building in 1927 and Miss Marion Elizabeth Chignell, daughter of one of the first directors of Ronuk laid the foundation stone on 28 July of the same year. The hall opened in 1928 lavishly equipped and with paintings by well-known artists. There is a main hall with many attractive features, oak panelling, a large bay window and balustrade galleries at either end. One of which contained an organ and a shallow stage area.

There is a fine mural by local artist Barry Huntbach, commissioned by the Council in 1971. They paid the artist fifteen pounds for the mural. The building also has two large committee rooms as well as a kitchen and a further large room on the first floor. The original organ built by Michell & Thyne has now gone but kept is the fine oak case, although moved to a new position. In May 1987, David Houlgate and fellow enthusiasts rebuilt a Compton-Christie 3/18 Theatre Organ from organ parts collected from around the country.

The Government Act of 1974 brought about boundary changes and the incorporation of Portslade into the Borough of Hove. Then in April 1997, the town merged with Hove into the single unitary authority of Brighton.

After extensive renovation works, there was a ceremony on 11 June 2014 to launch the reopening of the Town Hall. The new Mayor of Brighton Cllr Brian and Mrs Fitch attended the 12-noon meeting, which was followed by refreshments in the main hall.

The hall little-used now although recently refurbished, and today the Brighton & Hove City Housing Department uses the outbuildings as offices. There is a food bank operated on Fridays and Sussex Police also have their Neighbourhood Policing Team working in the building. The Main Hall renamed the Ronuk Hall is used for concerts and public and social gatherings.

Shoreham

High Street, Shoreham, West Sussex. BN43 5DA

Shoreham (Score ham) was in the Rape of Bramber and the Fishergate Half Hundred and the old town dates from pre-Roman times. This was one of the most important cross-channel ports in the twelfth and thirteenth centuries. King John (c1167 – 1216) chose the port when he returned to England in March 1199 with his army to claim the throne.

There was a Royal Arsenal in the town in the late twelve-century and several shipyards. The town built many vessels for the Royal Navy in the seventeenth century. King Charles II (1630 – 1685) used the port to escape, after the battle of Worcester. He travelled from England to Fecamp in France in the thirty-four-tonne coal brig 'Surprise', captained by Nicholas Tettersel in October 1651.

By 1828, there was an established steamer service to Dieppe in competition with Brighton and Newhaven.

The first railway line to Brighton opened in May 1840. This then enabled the carriage of goods from the port to the expanding towns along the coast. Later in 1865 saw the first lifeboat station at Kingston Beach. The cost of this was one hundred and thirty-three pounds.

With continuing problems with the French, the town built Shoreham Fort that was completed in June 1857. The cost for the work was above the original estimate at £11,685 10s 0d.

Shoreham airport was the first licensed aerodrome in the country with the initial flight from the airfield in 1910. The official opening was on 20 June 1911 with a flying school opening in 1913. It also claims to be the oldest purpose-built commercial airport in the world. It has the distinction of the event in July 1911 when Horatio Barber completed the first recorded cargo flight in a Valkyrie monoplane. During the First World War, a large army camp was set up Oxen Field for the 24th Division of Kitcheners Third Army. With good rail connections, a seaport and an airfield, this was an ideal position for training and disembarkation of troops.

The port was a leading South coast harbour with records of Bailiffs from the 1220s. In the early thirteenth century, this became both a borough (1295) with a mayor and a royal port appointed by King John in 1208. There are no official records of a mayor after 1346. This was a busy shipbuilding town in the seventeenth until nineteenth centuries and still today is a busy and successful port.

On 27 November 1703, the town suffered severe damage with many buildings destroyed, including the Market House, when a big storm struck the town. It was several years afterwards that Sir N. Gould and F. Chamberlin, Members for the Borough erected a new one. This building with an open ground floor area consisted of an oblong canopy of freestone decorated with Gothic ornaments, supported by eight columns, and stood in the centre of the town. The building was eventually replaced in 1823 by a brick structure, but later in about 1845 removed.

On the 6 December 1865, the town adopted the Local Government Act, 1858, and created the Local Board (1865 – 1894). Their first meeting was in 1866 with John Whitly Mardell serving as the clerk. The town's Board of twelve members who performed the civic duties of the town used to meet in Dolphin Chambers, High Street.

In 1875, they moved into East Street and the former National school building. This building, which formerly served as a Town Hall, is now part of St. Mart's Hall.

In 1880, the Local Board leased and moved offices into the old 1830 Customs House. This building in the High Street was built by George Henry Hooper and designed by architect Sydney Smirke, the younger brother of architect Sir Robert Smirke. This was later converted to the Town Hall in 1886 and opened on Lady Day, 25 March 1890, by Sir Henry Fletcher.

With the reforms of 1894 the Urban District Council (January 1895 – 1974) came into being with twelve members, which later increased to fifteen in 1910. Their first elected chairman was William Henry Harker, a local baker and corn merchant. The council also leased the old Customs House that was on the land of the Poole family mansion. In 1920, it became necessary to enlarge the building.

The building with a plain classical front, slate hipped roof with a stack to the left is two storeys high and with three bay symmetrical centres with one bay recessed wing to right. The entrance in the central bay has doubled panelled doors and with metal casement windows.

The Town Hall building has been since the 29 September 1969 granted Grade II status.

The fire brigade were housed on the western side of the building until the forming of the National Fire Service in 1941 when they merged with Southwick Fire Brigade. Soon after, they moved into the Butts Road fire station. They later moved to a new fire station in Stoney Lane, Shoreham on the 14 May 1955.

Shoreham extended its boundaries after the Local Government Board order of 1 October 1910 and the town renamed Shoreham-by-Sea. The Urban District Council then purchased the Town Hall in 1911.

There used to be a small arms shooting gallery in the basement. The Shoreham Rifle Club opened in August 1907 until 1968 managed this. Now there is a Bistro restaurant on the ground floor of the old building.

Later with the Local Government reforms in 1974, the town became part of the Adur District Council, combining the previous Urban District Councils of Southwick and Shoreham. There is a parish council but the Adur District Council essentially govern the town.

Adur District Council

The council was set up on the 1 April 1974 and comprises Southwick and Shoreham urban districts and the civil parishes of Coombes, Lancing and Sompting. Since 2004, they hold elections every two years with half of the members elected, after a change of the rules by the council. They have offices in Ham Road, Shoreham with other offices in Worthing Town Hall and Portland House in Worthing.

Adur Civic Centre, Ham Road, Shoreham-by-Sea, West Sussex BN43 6PR

As the council had been using five different offices scattered around the district, they decided in December 1978 to build a purpose-built Centre for the council. April 1979 saw the contract agreed and construction began. The costs for the contract were within the original estimate of £2.4m and works completed in sixty-eight weeks. On the 27 September 1980, Cllr Sydney Little, chairman of the council opened the new three storey red brick Civic Centre with its own Council Chamber in Ham Road, Shoreham. Nowadays with modernisation and cutbacks, most services have been moved to the Worthing offices in Worthing Town Hall and Portland House, Richmond Road, Worthing.

In June 2011, the council put the building and the 2.2-acre site in Ham Road up for sale, although they had been discussing the idea since 2009 but then it is was withdrawn. Later in early 2014, the site again was on the market. December 2015 and the council moved out of the Civic Centre and into new offices in the Shoreham Centre, Pond Road. The building will be demolished.

Southwick

142, Albion Street, Southwick, West Sussex. BN42 4AX

In the Rape of Bramber and the half - hundred of Fishergate, the Domesday Book of 1086 recorded the village. In Saxon times, the name of the village was 'Esmerewick' but by 1309, the name had changed to 'Suthewicke'. Remains have been found of a large Roman villa dating back to the first century AD on the edge of the town.

Part of the Steyning Union formed in 1835; Southwick Parish became an Urban District in 1899. There were twelve council members and the first gathering of the council was on the 24 August 1899. It remained so until the reforms in 1974. William Gardiner became their chairman, with meetings held in council offices in Albion Street.

Later the council bought land from John Hall further along in Albion Street. The Town Hall building composed of Southover brick and designed by George Walter Warr the District Surveyor. The building was faced with Bath stone dressing with castellated turrets. The costs were one thousand eight hundred and eighty-six pounds for the new building. The public hall could seat two hundred and fifty people. On the first floor was the Council Chamber and a bank occupied the ground floor. The local MP, the Rt. Hon. Sir Henry Aubrey - Fletcher presented the town in 1907 with a single faced clock. The council then arranged for the installation of the clock in the turret above the bank entrance.

The Urban District Council used the building from 1906 until the 1960s when the District Council offices moved to the seventeenth century Manor House in Southwick Street.

The Southwick Urban District Council had bought the Manor House in about 1965 and moved all their offices into the building in 1966. From 1974, offices of the Adur District Council were also in the Manor House. The old Town Hall by 1976 had become a warehouse and now houses small business offices.

On the 12 May 1840, the railway first reached Southwick. From 1909, there was a trotting track just north of the railway, until the Urban District Council purchased it in 1930 and turned into a recreation ground.

The Urban District Council also set up its own fire brigade with engines housed in garages in Butts Road, Shoreham. This later merged with the Shoreham fire service on the formation of the National Fire Service in 1941 and stayed at Butts Road. The Southwick St John's Ambulance Association, founded in 1929, used to run the Shoreham Police ambulance service.

There were plans in 1941 - 1942 for a New Town Hall but because of circumstances, there was no change. The last meeting of the Council was in March 1974 and now the town has lost all of its Council Offices and the Manor House use is only for private business. With the forming of the Adur District Council on the 1 April 1974, Southwick Urban District Council ended.

The new council now consists of Southwick and Shoreham urban districts and the parishes of Coombes, Lancing and Sompting and have their offices in Shoreham.

Steyning

The town called by the Saxons 'Steningham' was in the Rape of Bramber and the Steyning Hundred. In the Domesday Book, the town was the fourth largest town in Sussex and it received borough status in 1278. In the eleventh century, the town had a port on an inlet of the river Adur but this silted up over time. Steyning had been a parish since the reforms in local government of the nineteenth century and in 1980 after a parish meeting decided to keep its present status.

In October 1861, a railway station opened in the town. This was on the Shoreham to Horsham line but later closed in March 1966 under the Beeching plans.

Steyning never has had a town mayor but in the early years, a headborough held the position. He was the chief officer of the borough taking on the same duties of a mayor. The Vestry used the White Horse Inn and other inns in the village for town meetings, borough business and public meetings before the parish council was formed in January 1895.

At the parish council's second meeting in February 1895, they agreed to take control of the fire brigade. There are fire brigade logbooks dating back to March 1884 and good reasons to believe that the service was working earlier in the 1800s under Vestry control. The village fire engine a Merryweather was pulled by horses and housed in the Market House, 72 High Street. The nearby White Horse Hotel supplied and stabled the horses for the brigade. It was not until the 1920s, the brigade purchased a modern motorised fire engine.

Later, with a new engine supplied by Dennis Bros, the brigade moved and they garaged the appliance at the Coach House in the yard of the Chequer Inn. They later converted the building and on the 26 December 1935 officially opened this as the new fire station. In March 1961, the County Council built a new fire station in the High Street.

After the government reforms in the 1890s and the formation in January 1895 of the Parish Council, they elected Thomas Duke, a local farmer, as their first chairman. The first meeting took place in the National School in Church Street and their second meeting in the Town Hall.

From January 1895 until March 1896, the council used the Infants School for meetings and transferred to the Town Hall in August 1896. Regular meetings of the council were between 1909 and the mid-1950s held at the Town Hall, Jane Penfold Institute in Church Street or above the Steyning Gas Company in the High Street (1930, 1933-7).

38, High Street, Steyning, West Sussex. BN44 3YE

A locally formed company set up by a Col. Ingram, The Steyning Public Hall and Assembly Rooms Co Ltd, built the Town Hall in 1886. The costs were two thousand two hundred pounds. They bought a house on the High Street and asked a Mr Chalcraft, a local man, to build a hall in the garden behind the house. The building in the Georgian style with three windows has two storeys and a hipped roof of Horsham slabs. Built in red brick with two bays on the ground floor. The Petty Sessions and council used this for meetings and other public roles. The hall could accommodate four hundred people.

There is a stone four-centred doorway, with the date 1886 over the door. Since the 9 May 1980, this has been a Grade II listed building.

The County Council, in about 1958 purchased the Town Hall building as a permanent courthouse.

In the 1960s, construction began for the magistrate courts behind the Town Hall but these closed in 1995. The building was later converted and now is private housing and offices.

St Andrew's Hall, part of the former Gates's brewery in Jarvis Lane, was from 1928 used for public meetings and functions. Later in 1958, the council improved the buildings. The cost of works was seventeen thousand pounds and the hall superseded the Town Hall. Afterwards, in 1966, the parish council bought the building.

The Steyning Centre,
Fletcher's Croft, Steyning, West Sussex. BN44 3XZ

The parish council in 1993 built the new Steyning Centre in Fletcher's Court, to replace St Andrew's Hall, as their new home. In April 1993, Richard Woodman officially opened the building. As well as the council offices, there are two large halls and two conference rooms for hire for business or wedding functions. The clerk of the parish council is now Rebecca Luckin.

The Parish Council, Horsham District Council and West Sussex County Council now govern Steyning.

In 1894, Steyning Union divided. This then created the Steyning West Rural District Council and Steyning East Rural District Councils (1895 – 1928) in 1895. The Steyning parish formed part of the West Rural area.

This continued until the reforms of 1934. Later Steyning West Rural District Council transferred to the Chanctonbury Rural District and then later in 1974 became part of the Horsham district.

Both East and West councils met at the Union House, Ham Road, Shoreham, an 1836 building. The cost of the contract for the building was three thousand eight hundred and fifty pounds. Mr Elliot was the designer and W. Brooks the builder.

Worthing

In the Middle Ages, the town was a small agricultural and fishing hamlet known as 'Ordinges'. It was recorded in 1086 as being in the Rape of Bramber and the Hundred of Brightford. The village has had different names over the centuries and in 1288 known as 'Wortinges'. The first documented form of the modern name Worthing was in 1297.

By 1795, the town received its first of many royal visitors and started to expand into a popular seaside resort.

There was a naval signal station from 1795, and about 1809, construction started on the first coastguard station. A second coastguard station followed in the 1820s. Eighteen seventy-four saw the first purpose built lifeboat station at Marine Parade that served the town until 1929.

In 1803, an Act of Parliament, the Worthing Town Improvement Act passed to give Worthing town status. The new council then appointed seventy-two Commissioners to look after the municipal needs of the town. They first met at the Nelson Inn, South Street on the 13 June 1803. Later they met in 1812 at the Royal George Hotel, Market Street until they moved to the Town Hall. After the 1809 Act, a market was set up in the town with the first market held in 1810.

In 1845, the railway extended the line from Shoreham to Worthing and the town now had connections to London and the national railway network.

The Town Commissioners were replaced in 1852 and held their last meeting on the 17 July. The new Local Board had nine members at first that increased to fifteen in 1867.

They held their initial meeting on the 9 August in the Town Hall.

The Town Council, in turn, replaced them after Worthing and West Worthing became a municipal borough in August 1890. They held their first meeting on the 10 November 1890. After Queen Victoria (1819 – 1901) granted the town borough status, Alderman Alfred Cortis, the Local Board's chairman, was elected the town's first mayor. The original town clerk was W.H. Dennett, who had held the post of clerk to the former Town Commissioners.

The Old Town Hall, South Street, Worthing, West Sussex.

The building in South Street locally referred to as the Old Town Hall and built on land given by Sir Timothy Shelley of Castle Goring, opened with the first council meeting held in June 1835. Costs of construction were £1,215 8s 10d which included a fine clock tower. The architect was Ralph Jones, the town surveyor, and the contract awarded to Butler & Son (London) with the building in the Grecian style. This two-storey building, with a portico, contained a large room for public meetings, offices and a committee room and private apartment for the caretaker.

There were cells in the basement and a tower with a clock at its southern end. The bill for the clock dated 1835 and numbered 1205, came from Benjamin Vulliam and cost seventy pounds.

The face of the clock had four black dials with gold Roman numerals. In 1875, illuminated ones replaced these, as town residents could not read the time.

A local volunteer fire brigade was formed in 1813. A town resident presented a fire engine to them in 1815 that they stored in a lock-up until 1835 when it was moved to the Town Hall.

After 1839, and the Town Commissioners ordering a new engine, the Local Board in 1855 set up the town's first Fire Brigade. The fire service had offices in the basement at the rear of the Town Hall. With two manual engines and two fire escape ladders they were in the building from 1835 until their move in 1905 to the High Street. The Volunteer Fire Brigade was formed in 1869 with the amalgamation of the three services in the town. They later became the Worthing Borough Fire Brigade in 1893 under Town Council control.

With the developing town as a resort, in 1847, the Town Hall wanted extra offices. Under Charles Hide's supervision, the council enlarged the building and provided better courtroom facilities for the growing needs of the town.

Some years later, more office space was needed for the expanding town and the council held meetings between 1887 and 1921 in the newly built town offices in Liverpool Road. These offices had cost the council around two and a half thousand pounds. From about 1922, the council was also using offices in Chapel Road, as well as using Fairlawn and Tudor Cottages. This later was the site for a New Town Hall in 1932 - 1933.

This building in South Street served the town well until 1950 when the tower was demolished. The clock then was placed into storage, but later sold in 1970 for scrap. A few years on in 1968, Hall & Co demolished the building. The cost for this was one thousand and ninety-five pounds. The bell by Thomas Mears (1831) went on display in the newly built Guildbourne Centre.

After the West Sussex Review Order of 1933, the Worthing Rural District Council was formed on the 1 April 1933 and continued until the 1974 reforms. They held their regular meetings at 15, Mill Road, Worthing.

Chapel Road, Worthing, West Sussex. BN11 1HA

In March 1930, the Council invited competitive designs for a new building and chose Charles Cowles-Voysey, a London architect. Trollope & Colls Ltd of Dorking carried out the main contract with J. Brandon-Jones contracted for the detailing. Work began on 1 October 1931 and completed by the 31 March 1933, exactly on schedule. This work had called for the removal of the town's 1921 War Memorial. They positioned the memorial in front of the New Town Hall. The building also incorporates the Court House.

To the rear, is the Assembly Hall, a simple two-storey building in red-brick, with three stone relief panels in Art Deco style above the central windows, entrance doors. There is a plain canopy in 'Scandinavian' Modernist style.

The New Town Hall in Chapel Road is in the neoclassical style and was officially opened by Prince George, the Duke of Kent, on the 22 May 1933. The total cost of all the buildings and furniture was over one hundred and sixty thousand, under the original estimates.

The first mayor in this New Town Hall building was Alderman Harry Thomas Duffield.

Gillett & Johnson of Croydon, a company set up in 1844, supplied the clock and bell in 1932 and they refurbished the turret and clock in 1970.

The front of the building is in Neo-Georgian style with a centre and two wings of three storeys in red brick, a hipped slate roof and central Ionic Portico with the town's motto inscribed. The Clock Tower, with cupola and ball finial and eight Tuscan columns with plumed capitals, has a seven and a half-hundredweight bell that strikes the hours. The interior of the Town Hall has an impressively polished marble entrance hall and a staircase with elaborate bronze finished iron balustrade and a fine floor mosaic of the town's coat of arms. During the Second World War, the Town Hall played a major part in the town's war effort, coordinating the distribution of essentials for the protection of its inhabitants. For security, major items from the Museum and Library moved into the building.

In 1958, Keith Andrews & Co built an extension, the Richmond Room, to the Assembly Rooms for a cost of thirty thousand one hundred and twenty-seven pounds. In 1971 and again in 1976 remedial work was done on the clock tower and in 1978, ten thousand pounds was used for a facelift to the Town Hall. Since the 19 January 1982, the building has been listed a Grade II structure.

After the Local Government Act 1972, Worthing in 1974 became a district with borough status after the granting of a new charter. Nowadays Worthing Borough Council shares the Town Hall with Adur District Council.

In 1990 - 1991, Critchell Harrington (Chichester) built new Council offices at Portland House, 44 Richmond Road at a cost of £2.7m to provide additional office space. Her Grace Lavinia, Duchess of Norfolk, with the mayor, Cllr Hugh Braden, in attendance, officially opened the building on the 25 October 1991. Both Worthing Council and Adur District Council use the building. In 2013 major internal work was carried out by ECE Architecture of Worthing to provide a new customer service area which opened in April. The official opening of the new centre was in June attended by Brandon Lewes MP, the Parliamentary Under-Secretary of State for Communities and Local Government. During the renovations, it was necessary to remove the foundation stone that now resides in an office in the basement.

West Sussex County Council

Centenary House, Durrington Lane, Worthing,
West Sussex. BN13 2QB

Between December 1988 and 1989, the council opened Centenary House as the local offices for the West Sussex County Council. The cost of the project was £1.75m and took two years to complete. The West Sussex County Council chairman, Martyn Long, with the mayor and chief executive officer of Worthing Borough Council in attendance, officially opened the building.

This is a modern, flat-roofed five-storey glass and concrete structure typical of its period. The building is also home for the Sussex police service with police cells housed in the basement

* * * * * * * * *

Portland House, Worthing

5 Miscellaneous West Sussex.

The local government of a town uses a building for the town and civic business and these are not necessarily purpose built constructions. A town, with a town council and a mayor, using a particular building regularly for municipal meetings surely should call the building the 'Town Hall'. Some towns have had Town Halls in the past, but several of these have gone, due to various reasons, and a few small town councils and parish councils have taken over existing building for their meetings.

In West Sussex County, there are one hundred and forty-nine Parish Councils. In addition, nine Town Councils and one City Council and they are...

Arundel, Bognor Regis, Burgess Hill, Chichester City Council, East Grinstead, Haywards Heath, Littlehampton, Midhurst, Petworth, Selsey.

East Grinstead

In the Rape of Pevensey and Hundred of East Grinstead, a market town and ancient borough. The town, formerly a Saxon village, was in 1247 granted a market charter and borough status that it held for two hundred years. With the Reform Act of 1832, the town lost this status.

July 1855 saw the arrival of the railway to the town, a single track-line connecting to Three Bridges and the London to Brighton line.

In World War 2, the town became famous with the development of its hospital by Sir Archie McIndoe (1900 – 1960) and his pioneering treatment of RAF burns victims.

There have been municipal changes over the years. East Grinstead used to come under the jurisdiction of East Sussex, but after the boundary changes of 1974, it is now under Mid Sussex and West Sussex County Council jurisdiction.

In the seventeenth century, a Sessions House badly damaged during a trial in March 1684, when the floor collapsed required urgent maintenance. In 1686, they repaired the floor. This building was in the High Street and known as the Court House or Town Hall. The town lost the Summer Assizes, but the Lent Assizes continued here until 1799 when they moved to Lewes. They demolished the building in 1828.

After the Reform Act 1832, the Local Board (25 March 1884 – December 1894) was formed and Rev Charles W. Payne Crawfurd was elected as chairman. They held their first meeting on 30 August in London Road. In 1887, the Board built offices and a council chamber on the corner of Green Hedges Avenue and London Road.

The Urban District Council in December 1894 replaced the Local Board. At their first elections, Rev Charles W.P. Crawfurd was elected as chairman on 17 December 1894 and stayed in post until he retired in April 1897. The Urban District Council held its meetings in the old Council buildings, London Road (1894 - 1938).

In addition, after the Local Government Act 1894 the Rural District Council (1894 – 1934) was formed with W.V.K. Stenning JP elected as the first chairman at the meeting of 3 January 1895. Meetings were in the boardroom of the Workhouse/Poor Law Institute in Glen Vue Road from 1895 until 1932

This building was in 1859 designed by Frederick Peck and constructed by Peck and Stevens at a cost of five thousand six hundred and eighty pounds.

East Grinstead Urban District Council purchased and moved in 1922 to the old Hope Brewery, an 1839 building, at Norton House, London Road.

This building also housed the local fire brigade.

Council Offices East Court, College Lane, East Grinstead, West Sussex, RH19 3LT

By 1946, the Urban District Council acquired East Court for their new offices. East Court Mansion, now the home of the Town Council, is a fine example of a 1769 house, with a small park overlooking the Ashdown Forest. Built for John Cranston, a lawyer, the building is of red brick with three storeys and a basement. There are five bays on the long side and four bays on the short side with a tiled roof. They extended the building in 1906 with a new wing as well as a fine columnar entrance. The council restored the building in the 1980s.

Since the 28 January 1948, the building has been listed a Grade II structure. It is unusual in the fact that the Greenwich meridian line crosses the estate.

In 2011, the Town Council calculated that over four hundred and thirty-eight thousand pounds were required for the repairs and renovation to East Court to maintain this historic building.

By 1974, the town's status changed with the local government reforms and the creation of the Town Council. The position of mayor was established as a chairman headed the previous council. They elected John K. Andrews as the first mayor of the new council.

The town now comes under the governance of the East Grinstead Town Council, the Mid-Sussex District Council and finally the West Sussex County Council.

Littlehampton

The town, founded by the Saxons at the mouth of the river Arun, was by the eleventh century a small port with the inhabitants making a living from fishing and farming. It lies in the Rape of Arundel and the Hundred of Poling and mentioned in the Domesday survey of 1086 as 'Hantone'. Other names for the town were 'Hamm tun' and 'Hampton' but between 1610 and 1695, they adopted the name Littlehampton.

Beach Road offices.

There are reports that the name changed to distinguish the town from Southampton, locally known as Hampton. During Henry VIII's reign the town had a small shipbuilding industry, as well as the royal dockyards, but by the end of the nineteenth century had settled back to just a small port. At this time, many referred to the port as 'Arundel Port'.

Later in the eighteenth century, the town started to develop and by 1863 had a ferry service to Honfleur, Le Havre, and St Malo in France. It also had a service to Jersey. This helped to make the town popular as a holiday resort. This service closed in 1882 but the town continued to expand and today has a fine and popular marina and harbour.

Although there was a railway station opened, in 1850, called Arundel and Littlehampton some 1.5 km north of the town, it was not until August 1863 that a railway station opened in Littlehampton.

The lifeboat station opened in 1884 with the boathouse costing three hundred pounds to construct. Due to local conditions, the lifeboat station closed in 1921 and it was not until 1967 that the RNLI introduced a new service into the town. During World War 2, the town was home for the Royal Marine Commando Unit known as Thirty Assault Unit where Ian Fleming the author of the James Bond novels, was their, commanding officer.

After the Local Government Act 1848, there was a Local Board, holding their meetings at 27, Surrey Street. They governed the town from 1853 until 1894 and the formation of the Urban District Council. The UDC held their meetings from 1894 to 1933 at Town offices, Beach Road and later at the Manor House (1934 – 1974) in Church Street.

The Fire Service was officially set up in 1874 although there are records from 1833 showing the construction of a new fire engine house behind the High Street.

The Urban District Council in 1932 purchased the eighteenth century Manor House from Mrs Drummond-Murray and opened their offices in 1934. On the 21 March 1934, the council selected two local children, Joan Vera Strong and Eric George Laker, to perform the official opening ceremony. Lt. Col. C.C.R. Murphy, the council chairman, also accompanied them.

Manor House, Church Street, Littlehampton,
West Sussex, BN17 5EW

The building has brick and cement rendering and with two storeys is positioned centrally in the town. In 1830, the building had two extensions added. The main chamber for council meetings is twelve and a half metres by nine and a half metres. On the 21 August 1975, the building was listed a Grade II structure.

In 1998, the Town Council approached the Heritage Lottery Fund for funding for wheelchair accessibility to the building and was awarded half a million pounds towards costs. The council's contribution was one hundred and sixty-six thousand pounds and in 2000, there were extensive renovations of the building. The mayor, Anthony H Squires, attended the official reopening in November.

Since 1974 and the reforms, the town has its own Town Council with the mayor, Cllr Geoffrey J Hollis, and now comes under the governance of Arun District Council and West Sussex County Council.

Littlehampton Museum was founded in 1928, and after two previous homes moved into the Manor House in 1991, which it now shares with the Town Council.

Arun District Council

Civic Centre, Maltravers Road, Littlehampton,
West Sussex. BN17 5LF

The council was formed on 1 April 1974, after the local government reforms of 1972. It is composed of Bognor Regis and Littlehampton Urban District Councils and the Borough of Arundel as well as parts of Chichester and Worthing Rural Districts. There are twenty-two Parish Councils, seven Parish Meetings and three Town Councils (Arundel, Bognor Regis and Littlehampton.) within the governance of the new council.

In 1984, the council obtained planning permission for the construction of a new Civic Centre in Maltravers Road in Littlehampton. They had held offices in the Manor House but these were proving inadequate for the council needs. The contractor chosen was Conder Projects, with W. H. Saunders & Son the architects. Total costs were £2.7m and the building opened on the 26 October 1986.

The mayor of Littlehampton, Betty Newell, and Arun District Council chairman, Geoffrey McWilliam, accompanied Nicholas Ridley the Environment Minister at the official opening ceremony.

There was a large demonstration at the ceremony as many angry ratepayers were concerned about the expenditure of rate monies for the new building. They sprayed paint over part of the front of the building before its opening ceremony. With the help of volunteers, officials cleaned up in time for the formal opening.

Major regeneration and building works of the Civic Centre commenced in December 2010 - January 2011 with the official re-opening on the 10 January. The total costs were about two hundred thousand pounds for the refurbished Civic Centre Reception area and other improvements. Because of these works, both Church Street offices and the East Preston depot closed, saving the council thousand of pounds in maintenance and running costs.

Later in March 2012, the council installed one hundred and seventy-eight photovoltaic panels on the Centre's roof. This has reduced the council's electricity bills by up to four thousand pounds per annum and generated a small income by inputting electricity into the National Grid. Kingsley Eco Solutions of Ferring, Worthing carried out the installation at a cost of one hundred and one thousand pounds.

In March 2013, there was a major scare that asbestos could be in the building, but after extensive tests, this proved unfounded. Again, in 2014 there are external works made the outside of the centre.

Arun Council also has offices in Bognor Town Hall in Clarence Road.

Rustington

34, Woodlands Avenue, Rustington, West Sussex. BN16 3HB

Situated in the Rape of Arundel and Hundred of Poling, there has been a settlement here since the Bronze Age and possibly earlier. The Domesday survey of 1086 listed 'Nonneminster', which incorporated Poling and Rustington, as we know them now. After the coming of the railways in 1846 with a station at Angmering on the eastern side of the village, brick and tile production started, producing yellow clamp and red kiln bricks using the local clay.

The Parish Council was created in 1894, after the Divided Parish Act, with A. Heasman as the first chairman. The council used to meet at the Parish Church Hall and then moved to the Methodist Church Hall in Claigmar Road.

During 1918, but finished after the war ended, there was an American airfield just east of the High Street. Again, in the Second World War, there was a garrison of American and Canadian troops in the village. With the call to arms in 1940, the village hall became the local headquarters for the Rustington Home Guard

In September 1946 and again in September 1953 two world air speed records were established over Rustington sea front. The first set by Group Captain Teddy Donaldson in a Gloster Meteor Star and the other by Squadron Leader Neville Duke in a Hawker Hunter WB188.

The village also became the homes of Sir Hubert Parry the composer of the hymn 'Jerusalem', and J.M. Barrie the author of Peter Pan.

On the 1 January 1985, the parish council took over the management of the village hall and met at the old fire station (next door) in Edward Road, now Woodlands Avenue. James Linfield & Sons Ltd of Littlehampton had built the hall at a cost of just under three thousand pounds. The building's architect was J. Smith of Brewer Smith & Brewer, of Richmond Surrey. Mr C.D. Pinchin opened the hall on the 12 October 1938. After initial renovations, at a cost of about three and a half thousand pounds, further works were carried out in 1989, and the building of a council chamber.

On the 4 August 1989, the centre was officially opened by Peter Callaway, chairman of the Parish Council with Arun District Council chairman, Fred Lyons, and the mayor of Crowborough, Paul Scott, in attendance. The total costs of the improvements were one hundred and forty thousand six hundred and twenty-two pounds. Individual Service Builders Ltd carried out the works and the council arranged to spread payments out over a seven-step programme. The council moved their office on 11 August and the hall was renamed the Woodlands Centre.

The village had for some years toiled with the idea of becoming a town and set up a committee in May 1989 to consider the idea of forming a Town Council. Eventually on the 18 August 1989 after extended meetings, the Parish Council voted to become a Town Council. Peter Callaway the parish council chairman since 22 May 1987 was elected the first mayor of Rustington.

This situation caused a much-heated debate from many local residents, who felt that there had not been proper consultation and they demanded a local referendum. The council dismissed this idea but, within six months, the pressure to revert to Parish Council status had succeeded.

On the 23 February 1990, at a meeting held in the hall, with a vote of two hundred and three for the change and four against which sealed the fate of the town. Subsequently, on the 2 March 1990, the council voted to become Parish Council again.

This is not the end of the story, for on the 25 January 2000, the Parish Council elected to become a town again. The council nominated Mrs Alma Leonard, chair of the Parish Council, to the post of mayor.

This again caused massive disruption and anger within some parts of the community and they arranged for a referendum to overturn the council's decision.

On the 26 April 2000, the council held a poll and with a vote of eight to one finally sealed the fate of the Town Council. At a meeting of the Town Council, they decided on 22 May, to revert to Parish Council status. Mrs Alma Leonard resigned from the council on the 3 June at the meeting of the Parish Council, after eighteen years of service to the community.

For better or worse, Rustington is a village and for just over two hundred days had its own mayor, in fact, two mayors and that must make this a unique village in Sussex. The controversial decision to revert to Parish Council was taken, after a local referendum showed massive opposition to the Town Council idea and some very vocal and organised opposition to town status. The situation is unchanged today. Now it has reverted to Parish Council status again, under the governance of the Arun District Council and West Sussex County Council.

Selsey

Selsey (Seal Island), a once thriving village in the Rape of Chichester and the Hundred of Manhood, had the first monastery in Sussex in AD 683. There was a grand cathedral until 1081 when William the Conqueror (c1028 – 1087), ordered the removal of all cathedrals from villages to large towns. This move lost the town its prestige and income and Selsey has never recovered from this act. The town once an island is now part of the Manhood peninsula and the old Selsey cathedral and Deer Park is now beneath the seas. In the past, the village was renowned for its lobster, prawns and oyster fishing, regularly sending the catch to London and Brighton markets.

The local population welcomed its lifeboat station established in 1861 with the boat launching over the beach on skids.

There was a rail link between Selsey and Chichester between August 1897 and 1935 called the Hundred of Manhood and Selsey Tramways Company Limited. The cost of setting up the service was twenty-one thousand pounds.

Unfortunately, with its second hand rolling stock, this proved very unreliable and not very popular. The Chichester Observer in 1909 described the service as **'the noisiest and most rickety railway in England'**. Later the Tramways company name changed to the West Sussex Railway.

With the formation of the Parish Council on the 24 November 1894, they held their first meeting in the School Rooms at the Selsey National School, High Street. This later became the Infants School and on the 4 December, Newton Clayton a local farmer, land, and estate agent was then elected as the first chairman of the council. On 18 December, they held their first official Parish Council Meeting and Mr Clayton was confirmed as the chairman. Meetings were held here until 1906 and the opening of the new Mixed National School in the High Street in 1905, which is now the Medmerry Academy.

This was their home until the Annual Parish meeting on the 11 April 1938 and the move to the recently built Council School on East Street now renamed the Seal Academy. The first meeting in the new accommodation was on the 11 July 1938. Occasionally the Parish was holding meetings in the Church Hall.

The council first bought fire-fighting equipment after a parish meeting on the 7 December 1909. Mr A. J. Cutler, the ex-captain of the Chichester Fire Brigade, later formed a voluntary fire brigade in October 1911. They purchased a second-hand fire escape ladder from Thornton Heath Fire Station in October/November 1922 for the sum of ten pounds and it was ten years before they updated their equipment.

In the early days, the fire fighting equipment was stored behind Maidiment's Garage in the High Street before the building of a fire station in the 1950s. The buildings, a small garage and shed were at the far end of the High Street. By December 1964, a modern brick built structure replaced this.

After four years of fundraising in the village, a new Church Hall was constructed. On the 28 May 1924, Mrs H.W. Clayton opened the building with a concert program arranged for all the villagers.

The land originally purchased for one hundred and fifty pounds and the building costs did not exceed one thousand three hundred pounds. The parish council occasionally rented rooms for meetings until in 1977; the council bought the building for thirteen thousand seven hundred and fifty pounds.

The hall was renamed the Parish Hall and they stayed there until the formation of the Selsey Town Council.

55, High Street, Selsey. West Sussex. PO20 0RB

Selsey Town Council was formed in August 1995, after a resolution was passed by the Parish Council on the 14 July and held their initial meetings at the Parish Hall, with Michael Beal elected as the first chairman.

The Parish Hall, which is now the Town Hall, is on land that was formally occupied by the 'Inventive Factory' and originally part of the mousetrap factory of Colin Pullinger (1814 - 1894) the inventor. With his son Charles, they produced and sold over two million units. The council has provided a blue plaque for the building in recognition of the Pullingers.

The Council Chamber is fifteen feet six inches wide by thirty-eight feet long with oak panelling and parquet flooring and has the capacity to hold up to sixty persons. There is another large hall, which is twenty-four feet eight inches wide by forty-four feet three inches long with the capacity to seat one hundred and fifty persons.

These halls regularly host local events and collectors' fairs. There are kitchens and an exhibition hall, all of which are for hire for many activities as well as weddings.

Councillor Mike Beal is the current chair of the Selsey Town Council.

The governance of the town now comes under the Town Council and the Chichester District Council, which has offices in the Town Hall, and West Sussex County Council. In the past, the town was part of the Westhampnett Rural District Council (1895 – 1933) and the Chichester Rural District Council (1933-1974).

6 East Sussex

Records date back to 477 AD of the county, but in 1888, there were changes to the governance of the Sussex. The passing of the Local Government Act 1888 saw the formation of the counties of East Sussex and West Sussex along the traditional boundaries of the old Kingdom of Sussex. The previous county traditionally divided into units called '**Rapes**' but the County Councils superseded these. The first meeting of the new East Sussex County Council took place in Eastbourne in April 1889, but all subsequent meetings transferred to Lewes.

Bexhill

Originally, the village in the Rape of Hastings and the Hundred of Bexhill was set inland on a hill about half a mile from the sea and recorded in the Domesday Book (1086) as Bexelei. The town was quite late in development compared to its neighbours of Eastbourne and Hastings. Bexhill only started to develop as a resort in the 1880s and was not incorporated as a borough until 1902 by Edward VII (1841 – 1910). This then allowed the town to have a borough council and elect a mayor.

During the French Revolutionary and Napoleonic Wars of 1793 - 1815, the small village housed large barracks on its westward side. The erection of the barracks in 1798 catered for five hundred infantry and twenty cavalry soldiers. After enlargement, it was home for some five thousand troops, including three thousand of the King's Hanoverian Legions. The population of Bexhill at this time was just one thousand people. The Hanoverian troops were in barracks from 1804 until 1814 and with this influx of military helped the town to prosper. Subsequently, they dismantled the barracks in 1815.

Although the town can trace its history back to 722AD, when a charter was granted by King Offa of Mercia (r.757 - 796) it is most renowned for being the first resort to officially allow mixed bathing in 1901. The subsequent car racing along the sea front made this the home of British motor racing and Bexhill was the last town in East Sussex to be incorporated. Crawley in West Sussex was the last town in the county of Sussex to obtain incorporation in 1974.

From 1834 – 1884, the Battle Board of Guardians, who met at St. Peter's Vestry office, governed the town until July 1884 when they handed over control to the Local Board. Lt. Col. Henry Lane locally known as the 'Father of Local Government in Bexhill' was elected chairman and held that position for the duration of the Board. They met originally in the Assembly Room at the Bell Hotel until in May the following year when they moved to Dorset Cottage, Hastings Road. Due to an increase in members, they later moved the meetings to the Bexhill Institute in Station Road in 1893. The Board stayed there until the building of the New Town Hall.

The Local Board governed the town until the 1894 Local Government Act and the formation of the Urban District Council.

Town Hall, London Road, Bexhill on Sea,
East Sussex TN39 3JX

They held the last meeting of the Local Board in December 1894.

During 1895, when the town became the Bexhill Urban Council, it held its initial gathering on Friday the 4 January. The first chairman of the newly formed Urban Council was Lt. Col. Henry Lane, the chairman of the former Local Board who, unfortunately, died a few months later in April 1895. A memorial drinking fountain erected in 1898 in his honour is now on the green in the front of the Town Hall. Public subscription raised the money for the fountain.

Reginald Windsor Sackville, the seventh Earl De La Warr, wishing to turn the small village into an exclusive seaside resort commenced major development of the town in 1883. With the expansion and prosperity in November 1893, the Local Board acquired land (open fields) from landowner The Right Honourable Reginald Windsor, Earl De La Warr. This was for the New Town Hall and cost five hundred and eighty pounds. Henry Ward was the chosen architect, as he was a local man and had previously designed the nearby Hasting Town Hall. In 1893 – 1895, a local builder Charles Thomas of Western Road constructed the Town Hall.

The building is red brick and Bath stone structure in Renaissance style.

In a grand ceremony attended by the Lord Mayor of London, Sir Joseph Renals and his wife, the building opened on the 27 April 1895. This was a memorable affair, with the mayors from Eastbourne, Hastings, Lewes, Winchelsea and Rye in attendance. The fees for the building were above the original estimate and with furnishings totalled five thousand two hundred and fifty pounds. The cost of the Town Hall was humble in comparison to other buildings in the county, but Bexhill's building was modest in structure and has served the town well over the years. On the ground floor, there are offices and a fine stone and marble staircase leading up to the Board Room/Committee Room. This room is nineteen feet five inches wide by thirty-four feet long by thirteen feet high with stone fireplaces and a chimney at either end. Finished around the room is an oak dado. There are two further Committee rooms on this floor and a staircase leading to two spare rooms and an apartment for the caretaker.

At the rear in separate buildings, was constructed the fire station (1896 – 1971), a red brick and slated roof with space for two fire engines, hose reel, brigade room and stables for four horses. There was also a small mortuary and sheds for water vans, carts and other utensils. The brigade originally formed in 1888 with their first fire station in Endwell Road. They were taken over by the UDC and moved to De La Warr Mews in Station Road before moving to the rear of the Town Hall in 1896. Later in 1971, they moved to the corner of London Road and Beeching Road.

Some years later with more office space needed, the Town Hall had a further extension build in 1907 – 1908. The cost of this was four thousand six hundred and ninety pounds with Henry Ward as architect and W. J. Fryer the builder. They built a new larger Council Chamber as well as a public gallery and extra offices. There were further extensions to the rear of the building in 1937 and 1989 including the rebuilding of the tax office that stood on the Amherst Road side. In addition, due to lack of office space, the council purchased the houses adjacent to the Town Hall, one in July 1925 for one thousand five hundred and eighty-five pounds and the other in 1962 was bought for six thousand five hundred and fifty pounds.

It was not until April 1902 that Bexhill became an Incorporated Borough and Bexhill Borough Council elected Ebenezer Howard as its first mayor.

To celebrate the town's new status, the first official international motor races organised by the eighth Earl De La Warr and the Automobile Club of Great Britain and Ireland took place along the sea front on Whit Monday 19 May 1902. These continued until 1925 and the withdrawal of the racing permits. Soon after, on the 7 August 1926, the first British Grand Prix was held at the Brooklands race circuit in Surrey.

The railway arrived in 1846 with a small station on the Lewes to St Leonards route near the town. In 1891, a station opened near to Devonshire Square to serve the growing Bexhill community.

Later in 1935 with a budget of eighty thousand pounds, the town built the striking and impressive De La Warr Pavilion. After an international competition, the architects Eric Mendelsohn and Serge Chermayeff with their radical modernist designs received the commission for the works. The Duke and Duchess of York opened the building on the 12 December of that year. Refurbishment of the Grade I listed building began in 2005 with a £8m redevelopment program to restore the Pavilion to its original splendour.

After the 1972 Act, Bexhill joined the newly formed Rother District Council. Since 1974, the Bexhill Charter Trustees look after local Bexhill town affairs and arrange the election of the mayor.

Rother District Council

Due to reorganisation and the Local Government Act 1972, Bexhill Municipal Borough merged with the Rye Municipal Borough Council and Battle Rural District Council to form Rother District Council in April 1974.

Rother is one of three districts in the county of East Sussex. The council holds elections every four years and there are at the present time thirty-eight councillors. Within the district, there are two Town Councils and twenty-nine Parish Councils and one (East Guldeford) holding Parish meetings. The only borough status in the area of the Rother District Council is Hastings with its own Borough Council. The next tier of government is the East Sussex County Council. Rother District Council now has their main offices situated in Bexhill Town Hall, although previously they used offices in Watch Oak, Battle. In 2013, there were major repairs carried out on the roof of the Town Hall in Bexhill at a cost of two hundred and two thousand and twenty pounds.

Brighton

From little acorns this small Saxon fishing village once called Brighthelmstone or 'Bristelmestune' in the Domesday survey has developed into the City of Brighton and Hove (2001). A favourite of Regency royals to the capital of England's gay community, and to the election of the U.K's first Green Party Member of Parliament, the town has travelled far.

In the Rape of Lewes and the Hundred of Whalesbone (Welesmere) Edward II (1284 – 1327) in 1313 granted the town a charter to hold a market. In the early years, a chief constable, and headboroughs managed the town with appointed commissioners. They sat at a borough court dealing with the town's governance until the restructuring of local government. With the reforms of 1854 and the incorporation on the 1 April, the town became a Parliamentary and Municipal Borough. This had been a goal of the town as far back as 1685.

At the time of the Norman Conquest, this was an important town, but a town of two halves. One of the fishermen living under the cliffs and the other of farmers and labourers who were living on the cliff top (fourteenth century), and there was much conflict between the townsfolk. The fishing industry was well developed and fish sent to the London markets regularly. In a town without a harbour, there were eighty fishing boats in 1579. One hundred and fifty fishing boats in 1862 but by 1948, they had reduced to just forty-eight. Now the fishing industry is all but extinct.

Before the development of Newhaven, there was in the second half of the eighteenth century, a regular ferry service to Dieppe. Depending on the weather conditions, this could be a journey of seven to twelve hours duration. By 1817, there were up to nine sailing ships making the journey each week that later were replaced by steamboats. Before the erection of the chain pier that opened on 25 November 1823, the only way passengers could alight the ferries was by small rowing boats launched from the beach.

Like other towns along the South coast, it had suffered from raids by the French. In 1513 and again in 1545 saw the town burned and ransacked.

About 1592, the owners, Earl of Arundel and Lord Buckherste gave permission for the town to use the Town House by Black Lion Street and Ship Street to carry out civic business.

The building had a tower and a town clock with dungeons in the basement. The town expanded and by 1640 Brighthelmstone was recorded as the largest town in Sussex.

Times were changing and after the terrible hurricane of November 1703 that severely damaged the town below the cliffs, the town's fortunes took a different path. This storm also destroyed a third of the Royal Navy's fleet that were in the English Channel or sheltering just off the coast. Up to 8,000 sailors lost their lives and the Royal Navy fleet was decimated. It is recorded as the worst storm in British history. The storm of August 1705 was devastating and the sea demolished the 'lower town'. The town's wealth now faded until the arrival of Dr Richard Russell of Lewes who moved to the town in 1754. He was the saviour of modern Brighton with his beliefs of cures from the seawaters and bathing in Brighthelmston. The publication of his book in Oxford on the subject in 1750 helped to revive the town's prosperity.

In the sixteenth century, there was a Townhouse on the cliff top, but it suffered badly from erosion and possibly was demolished. There was a small two-storey, gable - fronted Town Hall on the west side of Market Street. Which formed part of the new workhouse that had been built in 1727. Vestry meetings and town business used this building. This Town Hall also housed a small cell known as the Black Hole. Soon the building became unsuitable for town meetings and from 1806, the Castle Inn later demolished in 1822 or Old Ship Tavern were utilised. In 1822, the Town Hall/Workhouse was purchased by the town commissioners and demolished the following year

The Society or Fellowship of Twelve governed the town at this time with a High Constable and headboroughs. After the Act of 1771, there was the appointment of sixty-four Town Commissioners (1773–1854) to govern the town and collect taxes. Later by an Act of 1810, the commissioners had increased to one hundred. The introduction of policing in the town was in 1812 although records show that in 1285 there was a designated town constable.

After the passing of the Brighton Town Act of 1825 on the 22 June, they appointed one hundred and fifteen Commissioners to govern the town. The Commissioners subsequently decided to demolish the Town Hall as the old building was becoming very difficult to carry out their business.

In 1827, there were plans to erect a New Town Hall on the site of the Market House (1774 – 1829) and a few years later, this was completed.

The construction of a new Market House in 1833 was on the site of the old Town Hall.

By May 1840, the first railway line to Shoreham opened. Closely followed in September 1841 with the opening of a direct connection by rail from Brighton to London, and this significantly helped the town to prosper. In 1852, the locomotive works opened with their first railway engine constructed later that year.

In 1850, the town Commissioners purchased for a cost of fifty-three thousand pounds the Royal Pavilion, originally built for the Prince of Wales in 1784, at a cost in excess of three hundred and fifty-six thousand pounds. By January 1851, it opened as a public building with an admission fee of sixpence to visitors. During World War 1, the building was a military hospital for Indian soldiers. From December 1914 until January 1916 they treated Indian Corps soldiers, but later also attended for soldiers of the Gurkha brigades.

The Royal Pavilion became a listed Grade 1 structure in October 1952.

With the millennium celebrations in 2000, the town of Brighton and Hove with Portslade were granted city status on 18 December 2000 and so formed the City of Brighton and Hove. This was after a long campaign known locally as 'The Place to Be' and led by Simon Fanshawe a local writer and broadcaster.

With the help of funds from the Lottery, the Brighton and Hove Council and local sponsorship the costs of the campaign had reached five hundred thousand pounds.

'It is official', the council received the documents known as 'Letters Patent' on Thursday 15 February 2001. The mayor Andy Durr received the documents at the Town Hall. Brighton and Hove then joined Inverness and Wolverhampton as the latest cities of the new millennium.

Bartholomew Square, Brighton, Brighton and Hove, BN1 1HG

After a competition in 1827 and the submission of thirty-five plans, Thomas Cooper, a town commissioner, was in 1830 the chosen candidate to design the New Town Hall.

Mr Doubleday put in a tender for £12,492 but the costs eventually rose after many delays to fifty thousand pounds. Thomas Read Kemp MP laid the cornerstone on the 15 April 1830. The Town Commissioners of Brighton held their first meeting at the Town Hall on 21 September 1831.

At their first meeting on the 7 June 1854 after the Charter of Incorporation on the 1 April 1854, Lieutenant-Colonel John Fawcett became the town's first elected mayor.

After the Local Government Act 1888, the town became a County Borough. They lost this status in the reforms of 1974 to be absorbed as a district in the East Sussex County Council. Then after many years of petitioning in 2000 – 2001, the town received city status.

The Town Hall with three storeys has two fronts, one on the North side and the other on the West side. Originally, the building was one hundred and forty-four feet long, one hundred and thirteen feet wide, and four storeys high. With three double porticoes composed of four fluted Doric columns, and a pediment in the Greek revival style.

The central police station (1838 - 1965) in the Town Hall had dungeons situated in the basement. The police cells were in use from the 1800s until 1967 and re-opened in 2005 as the Old Police Cells Museum. The Police Fire Brigade founded in 1881 had expanded by 1897 and had twelve police-fire stations around the town. By the following year, they moved their headquarters out of the Town Hall to Church Street.

The Brighton Fire Establishment was formed in January 1831 and a fire engine escape ladder and hose reels were stored at the Town Hall. Originally stationed at the Town Hall the Brighton Volunteer Fire Brigade created on the 14 October 1867, later moved to New Road. After the establishment of the County Fire Brigade in 1921, the Police Fire Brigade and Brighton Volunteer Fire Brigades were disbanded.

In 1855, the Corporation took over the responsibilities for the Town Hall.

In late 1897 – 1899, there was work to extensively alter and enlarge the building. Francis May, the Brighton Corporation's engineering surveyor did this at a cost of forty thousand pounds. The original staircase was poor, but after the alterations, there is now a fine 1899 staircase. Which rises in two stages straight through and then turning left and right at the end. The staircase then goes up to the second floor and a top lit galleried landing. The Great Room was removed and a new Council Chamber was provided as well as the basement converted to make a larger police department. During these reconstructions, the Council was holding meetings at the Royal Pavilion.

The Town Hall since 20 August 1971 has had a Grade II listed building status.

Like most large towns, the Town Hall is much too small for all the duties of a modern council and many buildings are utilised in the town for council business. In 1984 - 1987 two buildings around Bartholomew Square have been erected for municipal use, namely the four storeys Bartholomew House and Priory House.

Kings House, 4, Grand Avenue, Brighton and Hove BN3 2NL

Since late 1996, Kings House has been the headquarters of the Brighton and Hove City Council. They purchased the building from the South East Electricity Board for £4.5m and renamed the office block.

The listed building has a long history and was first constructed in 1871 - 1874 by Sir James Knowles, who designed the Grosvenor Hotel in London. John Thomas Chappell, the builder of the old Hove Town Hall in Church Road, assisted him. The building is on land from the Stanford Estate, in the previously known Queen's Gardens. Originally, known as the Princes Hotel it also contained private dwellings within the complex. Later in 1941, the Admiralty requisitioned the building and it became known as HMS Lizard. The South East Electricity Board occupied the office block from 1947. Architects Fitzroy Robinson Miller Bourne & Partners carried out major restoration work and an extension on the North side of the building in 1981.

This five storey building in yellow brick with a slate roof has a seven-storey pyramid-roofed tower with matching six storey corner towers. There are tall Italianesque brick stacks with overhanging eaves with moulded cornice from the roof. On the South side of the lower storey, there are three bays at each corner and metal balconies for the first and second floors. Since 31 May 1974, the building has had a Grade II building listing. Times change and in the last few years the council has decided to sell the building.

The running cost had reached five hundred thousand pounds a year for the upkeep. There are discussions on-going to move offices into the Hove Town Hall building.

Eastbourne

The earliest record of the village is in 963. The Domesday survey of 1086 records the village, as Bourne, although previously the name generally used was Burne. In the Rape of Pevensey and Hundred of Bourne, there are traces of previous Roman occupation found in the town. In the early fourteenth century, the town received a market charter. Later there was the discovery of the ruins of a large first-century Roman villa and bath in 1717 and 1841. In addition, in 1805, after a severe storm and discovered in the cliffs near the Wish Tower, Celtic gold bracelets were found. There have been two unfortunate naval encounters off the coast. One, the Battle of Beachy Head, on 30 June 1690 when the French defeated the Dutch and English fleets during the Nine Years War. The other battle in 1706 between the English and a French privateer called DuGuay Trouin.

The town is also reputed to be the first town to establish a system of sanitary certification for its houses with the Corporation supervising testing and inspection. The first lifeboat was a gift from John Fuller MP in 1822 and built by a local man Mr Simpson. It was a twenty-five feet wooden rowing boat with ten oars. Eighteen twenty-two saw the establishment of a coastguard service in the town. The railway arrived soon after on the 14 May 1849.

Built at the base of the chalk cliffs stands Eastbourne's famous one hundred and forty-two feet high red and white Cornish granite lighthouse, this cost twenty thousand eight hundred and fourteen pounds to construct. The lighthouse became operational on the 2 October 1902 after two years of construction and replaced the 1828 James Walker 'Belle Tout' lighthouse on the cliff top, which is still there today.

Later in April 1903, the world's first municipally owned bus service was set up with a red and brown livery. Frederick Bernard Fowler an engineer opened an airfield in St Antony's Hill in 1909.

He later purchased aeroplanes from a failing air school in Beaulieu, Hampshire. December the first 1911 saw the establishment of the Eastbourne Aviation Company initiated by Frederick Bernard Fowler with a share capital of fifteen thousand pounds. He set up business with Lt. Com. Frank Hucks RN and they opened the Frank Hucks Waterplane Company and the Eastbourne Flying School. They built aeroplanes and seaplanes and exhibited at the Aero and Marine Exhibition at Olympia in February 1914. At the outbreak of war, the Royal Naval Air Service requisitioned the airfield and set up a military flying school. During World War 1, they built over two hundred Avro fighter planes at the airfield factory on the Crumbles as well as seaplanes.

After the military handed over the airfield at the end of the war and then withdrew their presence, aeroplane construction ceased in 1919. The company was finally wound up in November 1932.

The council acquired the factory in 1926 but they only used the buildings for storage before they dismantled it. There were plans by the council to keep and extend the airport, but after many years of argument, they decided to use the land for housing development.

The Vestry that met at the church managed the town. Later the Eastbourne Board of Guardians was set up in 1835 following the Poor Law Amendment Act of 1834. As the town expanded John Haine, a local businessman in 1851 built a new Vestry Hall. The cost was two hundred and seventy pounds with the building situated on Grove Road; in July 1896, this became the library. The building later was demolished in 1902 to make way for the Technical Institute.

After the passing of the Local Government Act 1858, and elections in January 1859, the Local Board for the District and Parish of Eastbourne (1859 – 1883) took over most of the civic matters that the Guardians had controlled. They met at the Vestry Hall. However, by the 1870s, there was a demand for a Town Hall and the Local Board passed a resolution in 1874 to construct the building. This took ten years to come to fruition, due to the many disagreements and stubborn-minded individuals. This board was in existence until their final meeting on 6 November 1883. The newly formed Corporation superseded it after receiving the Charter of Incorporation of the Borough on the 16 June 1883.

Town Hall, Grove Road, Eastbourne.

The seventh Duke of Devonshire offered the town a piece of land called Stocks' Bank for a sum of three thousand pounds and the Board accepted the offer. This is now where the current Town Hall stands.

On 7 May 1883, the Local Board finally approved the plans submitted by William Tadman Foulkes of Birmingham. The Board selected a local builder James Peerless for the construction with the signing of the contract on the 9 June 1884 and work starting almost immediately.

On the 9 October 1884, Lord Edward Cavendish, the seventh Duke's youngest son, laid the foundation stone. The mayor, Alderman George Boulton with the mayor of Brighton in attendance, formally opened the building on the 20 October 1886. The Eastbourne Town Council met in the Council Chamber on the 25 October 1886 for the first time. The costs of the land, building and furnishings were forty thousand pounds and they used only the best quality materials. A Birmingham firm manufactured and installed the stained glass as well as another Birmingham company supplying the stone and wood carvers.

Originally, when they built the clock tower it was without a clock. It was not until July 1892 that work began on the installation of the four-faced clock with Cambridge chimes. Messrs Gillett & Johnston of Croydon carried out the works at a further cost of seven hundred pounds.

The company had supplied a clock to Hove Town Hall recently and was a well-respected and experienced company.

At noon on the 11 July 1892, the mayor (Mr Alderman Morrison) started the clock.

Twice a week the company would wind the mechanism manually, but in 1964, with the casting and the fitting of a new bell, there was the opportunity to add automatic winding and changes to the clocks' lighting. They still look after the clock to this day.

This is an asymmetrical building, with striking dark red bricks and moulded brick decorations, Portland stone dressings, a Westmoreland green slate roof and three remaining brick chimneystacks. The Town Hall is still a very impressive structure. The principal feature of the building is the off-central one hundred and thirty feet high clock tower. On the right of the clock tower is a wing of two storeys and attics with seven windows. To the left is a wing of two storeys and attics with four windows. Beneath the tower, there is a stone open portico and steps to either side.

The hallways, corridors and passages on the ground and first floors have marble mosaic floor decorations, and Minton tiles decorate the lavatories and cloakrooms. There are marble pilasters for the Grand Stairway of Hopton Wood stone, Main Hallway and Assembly Room. Some rooms have oak panelling and decorative plaster ceilings with floors of oak or parquet. The main meeting room is eighty-three feet long by forty-five feet wide and twenty-six feet high.

The borough police service was set up on the 5 April 1891 and incorporated in the building was the Police station and County Court with steps leading down to the cells. Since the 24 February 1994, the building has been a listed Grade II structure.

Under the Municipal Corporations Act 1882, the town, after incorporation on the 16 June as a municipal borough, established the Eastbourne Council in 1883. Their first meeting was in the concert room of the Pavilion, Devonshire Park on the 9 November 1883. At this meeting, they elected George Ambrose Wallis, the Duke's agent and an engineer and architect, as the first mayor of Eastbourne. All future meetings were at the 1879 New Hall in Seaside Road, until their move to the newly constructed Town Hall in Grove Road.

With the formation of the Volunteer Fire Brigade in 1884, the council purchased a fire engine, and by 1885, there was a fire station in Grove Road.

At a cost of six thousand two hundred and fifty pounds, a new building later replaced this. It was in the year 1912 that saw the purchasing of the town's first motor fire engine, at a cost of nine hundred and twenty-five pounds. This was in use until 1937.

In 1889, after the setting up of the East Sussex County Council in 1888 the new council held their first meeting at Eastbourne Town Hall on the 7 February. Lord Monk Bretton who had previously been president of the Local Government Board was elected chairman. All subsequent meetings were in Lewes, the County town after complaints from the Lewes councillors. They were very unhappy about the situation of meeting in Eastbourne and thought they should only hold meetings in the County town.

The town became a County Borough in April 1911 after the Eastbourne Corporation Act of 1910. Many years later, the Eastbourne Borough Council came into being in 1974, as a district within the Administrative County of East Sussex.

After the reforms of 1894, the Eastbourne Rural District Council was formed with G. Holmwood elected as their first chairman in January 1895. From 1895 until 1905, they met at the workhouse in Old Town. They then moved to Avenue House, The Avenue, and the home of the Board of Guardians. In 1931, they were holding meetings at 7, Cornfield Road and by 1932; they were at 4-5, Station Parade. By the East Sussex Review Order 1934, the council ceased and most of their area then merged with the Hailsham Rural District Council.

Eastbourne had its first elected woman mayor, Alderman Alice Hudson JP in 1926 - 28 and she was elected again in 1943 - 1945.

In 1961, the council agreed for R. Williams the Borough surveyor and H. Connolly the deputy Borough Architect, to build a new library and additional council offices. These were to be on the grounds of the old fire station and Technical Institute. Destruction of these buildings was caused by enemy bombings in an attack on February 1943 that left a large derelict area at one end of Grove Road.

The destroyed buildings, the fire station built in 1905 and Technical Institute built in 1904 left a bomb-damaged area that was an eyesore in the town.

The new buildings by Walter Llewellyn & Sons cost £193,611 for the council offices and £143,743 for the library.

The council rate and surveyor's offices occupied one part of the new building from late 1963. Because of recent cutbacks to police budgets and early closing of Police station's front offices, from October 2013, there is now a police contact point in the council offices. Sir Frank Francis officially opened the library on the 27 September 1964 with the mayor in attendance, although the library had been open to the public since the 6 April.

This is a modern building in Portland stone with a Lakeland green slate roof. The council has installed a plaque on the wall to commemorate the firefighters and others that perished in the air raid of 1943.

In September 1965, a one thousand one hundred pounds restoration and repair programme began on the Town Hall clock, the dial works and the reinstatement of the chiming and striking mechanism. In February 1994, the Town Hall became a listed building and remains a prominent and popular landmark in the town.

There are many repairs needed to the building today and the roof needs major work. After many months of discussion at council meetings Pellings LLP and Keepmoat Ltd made extensive repairs and refurbishment in 2013 to the building and roof at a contract cost of £692,266.

Hastings

The town has a long tradition of shipbuilding. It is a well-known town whose name is synonymous with William the Conqueror and the Norman invasion although with Saxon roots. Situated in the Rape of Hastings and the Hundred of Guestling, and recorded in the Domesday Book of 1086 as being a borough. The Battle of Hastings, which took place a few miles inland, gave the town the most remembered date in English history.

The expanding town became a Cinque Port in 1155 and next in importance to Dover if not more important. Hastings had endured terrible attacks by the French in 1339 and again in 1378, as did other coastal towns in Sussex and Kent. In August 1738, the town suffered a vicious attack by the French who burnt and sacked the town but it slowly recovered. As a seaside resort, the town has been developing since around 1775.

The old port is long since gone due to storms in 1287 and coastal erosion, chronicled in the past as seven feet per year.

Hastings Town Corporation had bailiffs and Jurats and the first recorded bailiff was William Cockesbrayn in 1275.

Queen Elizabeth granted the Charter of Incorporation to the town in 1589 and then a mayor replaced the bailiff. Thomas Hay who was bailiff at the time (1587 - 1588) became the town's first mayor in 1588 - 1589.

The Old Town Hall, High Street, Old Town, Hastings, East Sussex TN34 3EW

With the 1888 local government reforms, Hastings became a County Borough but this status ended in 1974 after the 1972 Local Government Act.

Later with the reforms of the Local Government Act 1894, the Hastings Rural District Council came into being. Henry Edward Cruttenden, a prominent local builder and contractor became their chairman. The council continued until 1934 when it merged into the enlarged Battle Rural District Council. Between 1895 and 1933, they were meeting at cottages at 11 Wellington Square. The Hastings Union owned these buildings.

There have been four Town Halls on three different sites in the town, with two of these still providing services for the towns' people today. The original late fifteenth century Court Hall used to be in the centre of Old Town on Courthouse Street. Existing records show that in 1601 - 1602, there were repairs made and the building of a new stairway and gallery. Later in April 1615, there was a consensus that there was a requirement for an additional new room to give extra offices for the Jurats. By 1702, they demolished part of the old Town Hall over the river Bourne. Records show a John Moore and Robert Bartholomew in 1710 then leased the building.

John Pultney and Peter Gott, members of parliament for Hastings funded the building of the New Town Hall in the High Street in 1700. The mayor at this time was Edward Milward (1699 - 1700). This building was in use until 1823 when they demolished and replaced the structure with a larger building.

The old Town Hall in High Street, Old Town was built in 1823 and replaced the earlier 1700 building. A two storey slate hipped roof building, supported on five low arches, with a market place beneath it and a small gaol, a cupola and clock. The costs were eight hundred and sixteen pounds to erect the building. Its main Council Chamber was forty-four feet by eighteen feet and fifteen feet high. Additionally, they spent a further sixty-three pounds for the ironworks around the market area at street level. The foundation stone was laid on the 2 June 1823 and the building officially opened on the 25 October 1823. In early 1848, the council renovated the building and it was in use until 1881 when it closed. The Town Council then moved to Queens Road. The council required extra space and in June 1868, new offices opened in Middle Street.

In 1749, the MPs for Hastings, Andrew Stone and James Pelham presented a fire engine to the Corporation.

The Corporation's own fire engine was later given to the Volunteer Fire Brigade, which had been set up in 1861. They stored their fire fighting equipment in the Town Hall from 1861 until about 1891. Since the 19 January 1951, the old Town Hall building has been a listed a Grade II structure.

There have been many uses for the Old Town Hall since the move to the new building. A Mr William H Reeves took a twenty-one years lease in 1906. It has been a police station, general offices, a furniture store, and library as well as a museum in March 1949. In July 1959, the building opened solely as the town's museum. It has recently re-opened after major refurbishment, funded with an award of one hundred and seventy-one thousand pounds from the Heritage Lottery Fund in 1999. The mayor Cllr Godfrey Daniel on the 14 October 1999 officiated at the opening ceremony.

207, Queens Road, Hastings, East Sussex. TN34 1QR

Henry Ward and contractor D.G. Jones of Gloucester designed and built the current Gothic style Town Hall in Queens Road that replaced the old Town Hall in Old Town. In March 1880 the sitting mayor, Henry Winter laid the foundation stone.

The mayor, Alderman W.F. Revill, officially opened the building on the 7 September 1881. Also attending the opening were the mayors of Sandwich, Winchelsea, Margate and Maidstone. This new building also incorporated the court and police station.

The cost of the building was twenty thousand pounds and there is a grand Gothic staircase, with marble handrails and a wonderful stained glass window. These feature the arms of King Harold, William the Conqueror, Elizabeth I and Queen Victoria. The Council Chamber has a Pitch pine roof and oak panelling and flooring with large Gothic windows. The courtroom had fine oak panelling, which the council sold after the court was moved in 1975 to a new building. It has been a Grade II listed building since 13 January 1999.

From 26 July 1940 until June 1944, Hastings suffered badly from air raids. The town experienced widespread destruction. Over four hundred and sixty-three houses were either destroyed or beyond repair. This had been the catastrophic result of eighty-five Luftwaffe air raids. During the Second World War, although the town had taken many evacuees from London, the council later decided to evacuate much of the town.

The early nineteenth century Summerfields school in St Leonards-on-Sea, a boys' Prep school (1903 – 1966) and previously known as Bohemia House (1824) was used as a temporary Town Hall. The Council's Town clerk and associated offices moved and held their meetings in the school from June 1940 until their last meetings on the 14 April 1945. Hastings Borough Council later purchased the school and grounds in August 1966 for one hundred and seventy thousand pounds, but the house was eventually demolished in January - February 1973. It is a pity that the council never converted the building and grounds into a new Civic Centre as they were using many offices in town for municipal use. The area now houses a new Police station that the Duke of Norfolk opened on 11 October 1972 and the Hastings court building that was opened on 10 October 1975 by Lord Widgery. There is also a new (1973) Fire and Ambulance station situated in Bohemia Road.

Today, there is still a thriving fishing fleet operating from the beaches below the old town called the Stade. This is Europe's largest fleet of beach-launched fishing ships and the historic fisherman's net stores and museum receives thousands of tourists every year.

The RNLI established their first lifeboat station in the town in 1858. There had been a service in operation from 1830, run by volunteers, from the fishing fleet. It was not until 1857 that a local lifeboat was available and this was stored in a boathouse at Rock-A-Nore.

There were plans for a New Town Hall and Civic Centre but due to the local government reorganisation of 1974, this did not happen. In 1996, there was a major renovation of the Town Hall with the outside works alone costing fifty thousand pounds.

Hove

64, Brunswick Street, Hove, Sussex

Originally part of the Rape of Lewes and Hundred of Preston, the town has developed well. From a small fishing village just west along the coast by Brighthelmstone to the independent town of Hove. Which is now amalgamated into the city of Brighton and Hove (2000). The village, as it was then, enjoyed a population of one hundred and one persons in the 1801 census, and with only one main street, Hove Street. There was a ring for bull-baiting, but this closed in 1810 after a bull escaped into the street. By 1831, a coastguard station opened in Hove Street next to the Ship Inn to combat the rising problems of smugglers.

Hove for some years had the title of West Brighton. This annoyed the residents but finally they developed independently as Hove although later in 1997 they merged to form the borough of Brighton and Hove.

The Brunswick Square and Brunswick Terrace Improvement Act 1830 set up twenty-one commissioners to govern the town although at this time Hove was just a small village, a mile to the West of the Commissioner's boundary. The Act of Parliament 1851 extended the Commissioner's jurisdiction to include Hove.

In 1858, the Hove Improvement Act was passed and after the 1894 Local Government Act, the Commissioner's status ended. The Urban District Council came into being the same year. With the granting of a royal charter on the 8 August 1898, the Corporation then governed the town with their first elected mayor, George B. Woodruff.

The Commissioners used a small building in the street that previously the police had occupied. These premises also housed the Police fire appliances. They later demolished this building and another adjacent building to make room for a New Town Hall. The Brunswick Square Commissioners authorised a Mr Russell to build the new hall in 1855 - 1856 at a cost of three thousand pounds.

The original Hove Town Hall, now a listed building, and known as the Brunswick Town Hall, was in Brunswick Street West. Incorporated in the building were the Police station and Police Fire service. When in 1873 the governors became the Hove Commissioners, they renamed the hall, Hove Town Hall. They stayed in the building until 1882 when they moved into the New Town Hall in Church Road. The three-storey, two bay building is still standing near the corner of Western Road. Hove Commissioners sold the building in May 1884 to William Charles Lake Bashford and it has had various owners since. The building achieved listing as a Grade II structure on the 24 March 1950.

The Old Town Hall, Church Road, Hove, East Sussex

The Commissioners purchased land between Norton Road and Tisbury Road from Mrs Ellen Bennett-Stanford of Stanford Estates at a cost of six thousand pounds for a New Town Hall. They signed the contract in June 1877.

The following year, they appointed Alfred Waterhouse (1830 - 1905) architect for the New Town Hall. A fine choice, as he had already designed the Natural History Museum in South Kensington (1868), and the Manchester Town Hall (1877). He later went on to design the red brick and terracotta Metropole Hotel (1890) and the Prudential Buildings on North Street, Brighton (1906). In addition, chosen for the construction works was a local builder, John Thomas Chappell. The council signed the contract on the 29 October 1879 and the building took two years and seven months to erect.

The Town Hall became a well-known landmark in Hove until a fire on Sunday, 9 January 1966 severely damaged much of the fabric of the building and left only the West side of the structure standing.

Alderman James Warnes Howlett, JP, with the Bishop of Chichester in attendance laid the foundation stone on the 22 May 1880. He also performed the formal opening of the Town Hall on the 13 December 1882. The final costs of construction were forty-three thousand pounds.

The building was a fine local red brick from the Sussex potteries at Keymer, Ruabon terracotta, Portland stone facings and a Gothic edifice. It had a forty feet high Great Hall measuring ninety-one feet by sixty feet with balconies on the South, East and West sides. There were left and right gables with five dormers each side between them and a tower. The grand one hundred and twenty feet clock tower contained a twelve-bell carillon and clock with four dials. Gillett & Bland of Croydon supplied the clock and bells, which weighed nine tons at a cost of £1,576 10s 0d. They played fourteen different tunes. The hour bell, weighing thirty-six hundredweight, was given the name the Howlett bell, in honour of Alderman J.W. Howlett, JP (1828 – 1911). Messrs Salviati, Burke and Co supplied at a cost of one hundred and eighty pounds, the mosaic clock dials that had a diameter of seven feet.

The Great Hall could seat two thousand people and was the largest capacity hall anywhere in Hove or Brighton.

There was a police station (1882 – 1964) with five cells as well as a police fire station in the basement. This contained one fire escape and two hose reels (1866 - 1899). Situated below the Great Hall, this caused some problems, as there was a steep slope up to the street.

In 1894, Messrs Crompton & Co carried out the work of installing electric lights for the Town Hall. The cost of the works was sixteen hundred pounds.

A few years later in 1897, the Town Hall hosted its first film show and continued showing films until the first picture theatre opened in the town in 1910.

Later in 1911, Messrs Gillett & Johnson, as they now had become, illuminated the clock dial plates at a cost of three hundred pounds, which James W Howlett paid for. In 1921, there was remedial work carried out on the wire connections of the bells in the tower at a cost to the council of forty-eight pounds and ten shillings.

In the Great Hall, there was a concert organ built-in 1896 - 1897 by Henry Willis (1821 – 1901) of Camden Road, London. Due to modernization plans for the building, the council sold the organ in 1959 for fifteen hundred pounds to the Haberdashers' Aske's School at Elstree as it was under used.

Sadly on the 9 January 1966, a fire attended by seventy firefighters, twelve pumps and turntable ladders, destroyed most of the Town Hall including the Great Hall and the Council Chamber. Walter Llewellyn & Sons from Eastbourne demolished the last remaining parts of the original building between October and November 1971.

After the fire in the previous Town Hall and many years of debate on whether to build a New Town Hall or repair the old building, a competition was held for a design for the replacement building. The council moved offices to the museum building Brooker Hall. They used these as a temporary town hall until completion of the new municipal building.

Norton Road, Hove. BN3 4AH

The council chose John Wells-Thorpe, a local architect of Gotch & Partners to expedite the new building project, with a tender of £1.4m although the final cost was nearer to £2.2m. Contractors Walter Llewellyn & Sons of Eastbourne started the works, which were completed in 1974.

Lord Rupert Nevill officially opened the building on the 5 March 1974. In 1991, they added a new extension, as the council needed extra office space for the Registrar, Tourist centre and Citizen's Advice Bureau.

This is very much a modern building with reinforced concrete and nine hundred unpainted cladding units. The units constructed with Derbyshire Spar and Hopton Wood stone and huge panes of bronzed Spectrafloat glass make this a prominent building in Hove. At the lower levels, they used Clee Hall aggregate and panelled the interior in Wych elm with Finnish brickwork. Part of the design is a hanging garden with indoor plants over the Western entrance.

Since 1978, the building has had repairs and extra offices built over the former quadrangle. The latest works being in 1991 with the building of extra offices in the undercroft at a cost of three hundred and eighty thousand pounds. The mayor Cllr Audrey Buttimer performed the opening ceremony on the 14 January 1992.

Whilst the building was being renovated in April 2015 there was a large fire on the roof. It is believed that this was caused by the solar panels and there were no casualties.

This was not a very popular building design, but over the years, locals have begun to appreciate the building as a fine example of 1970s architecture.

Lewes

The Old Town Hall. Lewes, East Sussex.

This town is the county town of East Sussex and has been an important area since the Saxon days. The spelling of the town name then was Leswes. Lewes had two mints and was mentioned in the Domesday Book 1086 as being a borough. It was renowned for its iron works and independent radical minded residents. In the Rape of Lewes, there has been some type of municipal government for many years in the town.

King Stephen in 1148 granted a charter to the town, and a body called the 'Fellowship' performed the office of government.

There has been a parliamentary borough since 1295. In 1147, Rainard de Warenne restored the merchant gild and the Fellowship formed in 1149 with limited powers, headboroughs were responsible for the collection of taxes. Later town constables were appointed and the first in 1544 were Clement Puggesley with another, a Joseph (surname unknown)? The Fellowship consisted of twelve members, assisted by the Council of Twenty-four, and was active until 1663. After the 1806 Act of Parliament known as the Town Act, they appointed Commissioners to administer town affairs.

The Lewes Town Council on 8 November 1881 held their first meeting after incorporation of the town on 17 June of that year.

The first railway station to open in Lewes was in June 1846 with a connection to Brighton. The following year, there were connections to Hastings and Newhaven.

There used to be a line between Lewes and Uckfield, part of the Wealden Line, but this closed in May 1969. There is now an active campaign to reopen this line.

During World War 1 and World War 2, the County Hall and Town Hall were used to billet soldiers before they embarked from Newhaven for service in France.

The old Town Hall or Sessions House was a stone quoined, brick edifice with courtrooms on the first floor and an outside staircase at the west end.

The building used to stand in the middle of the High Street close to the White Hart Inn. Designed and built by John Morris in 1761 to replace an earlier wooden structure built about 1565 as a Sessions House and Town Hall. The building had major repairs done both in 1665 and again in 1713 when the Constables spent £36 10s 7d altering the Sessions House.

This building was in use for about fifty years. The Sessions House was some fifty-four feet long and twenty-four feet wide with a large octagon copula in the centre of the roof.

Later the council decided to auction the building. This was due to it becoming a nuisance being in the middle of the road and in need of substantial repairs. As the structure did not reach its reserve price, the auctioneer, George Verrall bought the building. The price paid was four hundred and sixty pounds on the 29 May 1810. Amon Wilds, a local builder, later bought the building for four hundred and fifty pounds. Soon after in 1812 the building was taken down.

The White Hart Inn was used for official meetings until the Town Council obtained special permission by an Act of Parliament to use the newly erected County Hall (1808 – 1812), by John Johnson. All further official town business took place in the new hall, as they did not have their own designated building to carry out the town's affairs. This continued until 1890. The building in the High Street, also known as the Shire Hall and constructed in Portland stone is still in use today as the County Court building.

Lewes

High Street, Lewes, East Sussex. BN7 2QS

The site where the present Town Hall now stands was in the fourteenth century owned by monks of the Southover Priory. Then with the dissolution of the monasteries by Henry VIII in 1537, the freehold was the site of the Star Inn. Until 1890, the Star Inn remained one of Lewes's leading hostelries. The 1840s saw the construction of a new capacious Corn Exchange built adjacent to the Inn.

In July 1883, W.J. Smith the owner of the Star Inn offered the building and freehold to the council for five thousand one hundred pounds. After early opposition, it took the council until 1890 to reach a decision to then purchase the Star Inn and Corn Exchange. They offered a reduced sum of four thousand and one hundred pounds and this was accepted. The building then became the Town Hall.

Lewes town received its Charter of Incorporation in June 1881. On Wednesday 9 November 1881, the first meeting of Lewes Borough Council (1881 – 1974) took place in the Record Room of the Market Tower, Market Street. The council stayed there until they moved to the New Town Hall in 1893. Lewes's first elected mayor was Wynne Edwin Baxter who had been the last High Constable. He was a solicitor and Coroner for Sussex and among others conducted inquests into the Whitechapel murders, as well as the Joseph Carey Merrick (the Elephant Man) case.

The building was remodelled by Samuel Denman of Brighton and the kitchens and stable-yard were demolished for the new Assembly Room. The cost was about seventeen thousand pounds and the mayor, Edward Hillman, officially opened the building on 9 November 1893. The building has red brick and terracotta decoration, and is on three storeys with eight bays. There is a fine carved oak Jacobean staircase (1620) leading to the upper floor. This came from the Thomas Sergison dismantled mansion of Elizabeth Slaugham Place. The council chamber is forty-nine feet by twenty-two feet by thirteen feet nine inches and panelled with Elizabethan oak panelling conserved from the old building. In addition, there is an undercroft dating from the fourteenth century with an arch and tunnel vault. In 1913 - 1914, there were new council offices built and since the 25 February 1952, the building has been Grade II listed.

In 1974, saw the creation of Lewes Town Council, successor to the Lewes Borough Council, residing at the Town Hall. Like many local councils, they have several rooms to hire for weddings or business seminars. The council consists of eighteen elected members and the mayor and a town clerk lead them. There are eight full-time employees with a further seven part-time staffs.

The Town Hall has changed hands many times over the years firstly purchased in 1890 and then in 1974 the ownership passed to the newly created Lewes District Council. Later in February 1999, Lewes Town Council bought the building.

In 2006 - 2007, major works commenced at the Town Hall for access for the disabled. The estimated costs of this work were one hundred and ten thousand pounds. Recently, in 2013, the council commissioned an inspection of the South façade of the Town Hall. They appointed BLB Surveyors Ltd of Brighton to ascertain work and costs of repairs. A budget agreed and thought sufficient was one hundred and fifty thousand pounds with works commencing in 2015. Clarke Roofing Southern Ltd carried out the works.

Southover House, Southover Road, Lewes, East Sussex. BN7 1AB

After the 1972 Local Government Act, in April 1974 saw the formation of the Lewes District Council. The new body was created from the recently abolished local authorities, namely the Chailey Rural District, Lewes Borough, Newhaven Urban District and Seaford Urban District. Councillor R.H. Yarrow MBE was elected their first chairman.

Initially, the council moved into Lewes House, an early eighteenth-century building, at 32 High Street (School Hill) the home of the now defunct Chailey Rural District Council (April 1934 - April 1974).

Later, on the 23 December 1997, the council purchased Southover House. It was not until 1999 that most of the staff moved into the building.

In July 2013, the council appointed ECE Architecture of Worthing to carry out improvements. The ground floor area was then closed to the public for improvements and a new refit for better access. When the works were finalised the remainder of the staff in Lewes House joined their colleagues. Offices in Lewes House are still used by the council.

Due to economic changes in 2015, Lewes District Council and Eastbourne Borough Councils have agreed to share the post of Chief Executive. Robert Cottrill the Chief Executive of Eastbourne Borough Council will take up this position. It is hoped that this action will save the councils £2.9m and the sovereignty of each council will be retained.

East Sussex County Council

As we are in the county town of Sussex, we also have the County Hall, with the County Council being the top tier of local government. As with other older towns, there has been more than one building used for this purpose and some of them still survive.

On the 1 April 1889, after the Local Government Act 1888, the town became the headquarters of the newly established East Sussex County Council. Meetings of the East Sussex County Council, after the initial one in Eastbourne, when the original fifty-one members voted Lord Monk-Bretton as chairman, were held at the County Hall in High Street Lewes (April 1889).

Later, meetings took place at the Town Hall in Lewes. Pelham House in Lewes held meetings from November 1938 until October 2003. These took place in a purpose-built chamber until 2003 when the council sold Pelham House.

County Hall now Law Courts, High Street, Lewes, East Sussex BN7 1YB

There had been plans drawn up in 1801 for a new building on the North side of the High Street. The Quarter Sessions commissioned John Johnson (1732 – 1814) architect of Camden Town for the plans. He had previously been involved with the building of the Chelmsford Shire Hall, but these plans never came to fruition.

After a meeting in February 1808, they decided to apply for an Act of Parliament. This was for permission to remove the old Sessions House and purchase land and to construct a new court building. Subsequently with the approval of the Act, and the re-adoption of the old plans, the East Sussex Quarter Sessions purchased the freehold of land owned by the Earl of Chichester. The price paid was two thousand pounds. Several houses had to be demolished for the new County Hall, which gave it a sixty-foot frontage onto the street. Although the elderly John Johnson had drawn up the original plans the building committee appointed two others to assist in the building of the new hall. They were William Balcombe Langridge and John Cowper, a local architect and builder, as clerk of the works. During construction, they realised that the original plans planned for a seventy-foot frontage to the street. Additional land was required.

After much discussion, they purchased the freehold property owned by William Miles for one thousand two hundred and fifty pounds.

Built in 1808 – 1812, after the move from the shared structure in the middle of the road, the building stands on the North side of the High Street. Originally built for the Court of Quarter Sessions it then passed to the newly formed County Council in 1889. This building is still in use today and houses the County Court. The two-storey building has a Neo-Classical façade in Portland stone and a slate roof, with high relief Coade stone panels manufactured by Coade & Sealy of Lambeth. It had an open ground floor, with an open colonnade in five bays, assembled with a middle loggia of Tuscan columns. With the major courtroom on the first floor, a large room sixty feet by thirty feet lighted by tall windows. Unusually prisoner cells were in the back yard.

The new County Hall finally opened in 1812 under the permitted budget of £15,000 for the total costs of building works at £12,440 16s 10d. These included the mason's cost, Mr Latter Parsons of Lewes, of nearly £1,000 and site costs of £4,228 10s 3d. There was a proviso in the Act that the Lewes Borough could use the building. Since the 25 February 1952, the court building has been listed a Grade II structure.

In 1890-1892, there were extensive alterations to the County Hall at a cost of seven thousand three hundred and ninety-four pounds plus two hundred pounds for electric lights. Again, in 1901, there were further works with extensions to the building. The Council Chamber is sixty feet by thirty feet and used exclusively by the County Council.

By 1907, other buildings in the town were utilised by the council including offices in Fisher Street. Due to the expansion of the town and a shortage of office space in the mid-1920s, the council decided to purchase more properties. Fifty thousand pounds was set aside for the acquisition of Castlegate House, 180 and 180a High Street. In addition, they purchased Pelham House in St Andrews Lane in September 1928 for seven thousand five hundred pounds. In 1930, the council acquired Newcastle House. The architect, Sir Reginald Blomfield, assisted by E. A. Verger built the new extension. Again, in 1957 major works to the front of the building were required after masonry fell into the street. Appointed for the works was C & C. J Pannett of Lewes under the supervision of Messrs Szerelmey Ltd. The total costs of the contract for the works were £6,827 6s 1d.

Lewes

Pelham House, St Andrew's Lane, Lewes, East Sussex BN7 1UW

East Sussex County Council purchased the house in September 1928 and the clerk of the Council moved into Pelham House in 1929.

The building was originally built on land that was formerly the property of John Cotmot, the churchwarden of St Andrews. In 1579, George Goring a previous MP for Lewes purchased the house and land and spent two thousand pounds on his new stone mansion, after demolishing the old dwelling. The building has passed through many owners including the Pelham family who had occupied the house from 1653 for over one hundred and fifty years.

Thomas Pelham and William Campion remodelled the house between 1725 and 1812. A partially rendered, red brick building, and a hipped slate roof and four brick stacks with a twentieth-century brick extension. Further two storeys with attics and a central glazed doorway in arched surround with a triangular pediment. Pelham House became a Grade II listed building on the 25 February 1952.

Within a short time, the Council was holding meetings at the Town Hall as the Surveyors Department occupied the Council Chamber. There were plans to extend Pelham House and in 1938, the Council added a major extension. This was to house a Council Chamber, committee rooms, offices and storerooms. The first meeting of the Council took place on 8 November 1938 in their new council rooms.

During World War 2, the Civil Defence headquarters for the county was in the basement of Pelham House. The house was in use by the East Sussex County Council until 2003 and then sold in 2004 to a private business and converted into a hotel and conference centre.

County Hall, St Anne's Crescent, Lewes, East Sussex. BN7 1UE

By 1961, council office and staff were scattered all over Lewes in thirteen different buildings and there was an urgent need for a central office. Approval of the final plans for a new hall in 1964 and a tender of seven hundred and seventy-six thousand pounds were accepted. County architect, Jack Catchpole had the responsibility for the design and J. Lawson & Co. Ltd of London was the builder of the new three-wing building with linked lower units.

Over the entrance there is an excellent large twelve-metre, fibreglass painted rectangular relief. William George Mitchell constructed it from eleven separate panels. The total cost of the building was more than £1m including furniture and equipment. HRH The Duchess of Kent opened the new County Hall on the 31 October 1968 with the dedication given by the Bishop of Chichester. At first, the Council held meetings in Pelham House but since 2003, all meetings are in the new Council Chamber in County Hall although offices in the eighteenth century Lewes House are still in use.

This is a quotation from the South Downs National Park Authority, Planning Committee on 12 December 2011 re a proposed extension to the Lewes Conservation Area.

"It is accepted that the County Hall building…. is an unattractive, visually dominant building of no architectural merit, whose demolition would be welcomed by most Lewes residents. However, there are plenty of examples of similar buildings of the same era, which are included in the conservation area of a major historic town or city, including Canterbury, Exeter and Lincoln. Designation of a conservation area would not prevent the redevelopment of the County Hall site but would encourage the construction of well-designed new buildings which would fit in with the surrounding landscape and not dominate this part of the town".

It is not surprising that in 2014 there was discussion about moving council offices out of Lewes.

Pevensey

The Celts, Romans and Saxons inhabited the village many years before the Norman landings in September 1066. The village was located in the Pevensey Rape known also as the Lowey or Liberty of Pevensey. It was the Romans in the fourth century who first built a fort in Pevensey as part of their series of 'Saxon Shore Forts' that covered Kent, Sussex and Hampshire in the South of England. Pevensey port was a very important and busy gateway to Normandy. This was the place where William, Duke of Normandy, landed in September 1066. The port was still in use in the reign of Henry III (1207 – 1272). Over time, the port has disappeared due to the sea receding and the original outlet becoming choked up by silt (1650–1700). A Trinity House report of 1698 stated that the haven *'was closed and irrecoverably lost'*.

The Normans started a small mint in the Castle and this was in use until 1240. Pevensey was also a partner Cinque Port with Hastings.

High Street, Pevensey, East Sussex. BN24 5LF

Pevensey is reported in ancient records to have had a mayor and Corporation before the Normans landed and indeed had its own Corporation until 1866. King John granted a royal charter to the town in 1207 and the Pevensey Corporation governed the town.

After the Municipal Corporations Act of 1883 saw the Corporation dissolved in March 1886 and the town lost its borough status and is now a village with a parish council. For a short time, a local committee looked after the Corporation affairs. The Charity Commissioners in March 1890 proposed that the newly formed Pevensey Town Trust run by volunteers should manage the residual property of the Corporation. The Trust is still active today. Unfortunately, a devastating fire in 1886 destroyed most of the early records of this time.

It was in 1851 that a railway station opened and served both Pevensey and Westham villages. The Pevensey Fire Brigade formed in 1912 and stationed at the rear of the Smugglers public house in the High Street. They stayed here until the move in the 1940s to Church Lane.

The municipal building originally a thirteenth-century structure and was possibly built on an even earlier building. Rebuilt in 1540, this white plastered building on two storeys with tiled roof, two main rooms and steps leading up to the first floor is now a museum. It stands on ground nineteen feet by twenty-three feet.

Situated on the first floor of the Town Hall, the Court Room is eighteen feet by fourteen feet. A gaol is on the ground floor with two cells. There is a small area some eight feet by six feet for exercising at the rear. An extension at the back of the building is the home for the Beagle that is now in private ownership. There were a further six cells built-in its cellar. The courtroom and some of the cells and exercise yard are still intact and the building is reputed to have been the smallest Town Hall in England. With the dissolution of the borough in 1886, its use as a Town Hall ended. The building was used for storage and neglected until the reformed Pevensey Town Trust in the 1960s took over the care of the Town Hall. They then converted the building into a museum. Since the 30 August 1966, the hall has been a listed Grade II building.

In 1940, during the Second World War, Pevensey Castle was fortified and the cots in the cells of the Town Hall were zinc lined. This meant that the cells then could be utilised as a mortuary. After a German pilot crashed his plane near the village, local people managed to capture him. The villagers escorted him to one of the tiny cells of the gaol until he was collected some hours later by the army. A Parish Council, Wealden District Council and East Sussex County Council, now govern the village of Pevensey and Pevensey Bay.

Rye

Even before the Domesday survey, Rye was a borough and an expanding town in the Rape of Hastings and Hundred of Goldspur. King Stephen set up a royal mint in 1141. The inclusion of the town within the Confederation of the Cinque Ports in 1191 showed how important and prosperous the town was becoming. Rye first received rights of governance in 1289. It was a corporation by prescription and had its own mayor and Jurats. This remained until 1973 when the Local Government Act was enforced. The first recorded mayor was Henry de Rakele in 1289 although it is possible there could have been earlier mayors in office.

The town has had a lifeboat since 1803 and the misfortune of one of the RNLI's histories worst lifeboat disasters. On the 15 November 1928, seventeen members of the "Mary Stanford" lost their lives.

After the Norman Conquest, Rye developed and became a major port and a member of the Cinque Ports. The French from 1339 through to 1448 raided the town regularly. Rye has also suffered severely by storms and the silting up of its harbour and erosion by the sea. This erosion has destroyed large parts of the East of the town over the years. The great storm of 1287 changed the course of the river Rother (Limene). With the sacking of the town in 1377 and again in 1447 by the French, this contributed to the decline in the town's fortunes.

The French, on a raid in 1377, attacked and burnt down the first Town Hall building. While awaiting a New Town Hall, the Corporation used the Ypres Tower for town business. Later the Tower became a jail, and now it is the town's museum.

6, Market Street, Rye, East Sussex, TN31 7LA

Between 1514 and 1515, the Corporation built a New Town Hall. By 1742, it was in such a dilapidated state the Corporation decided to demolish the building.

For the new hall, the Corporation had to borrow money from two of its members, Sir John Morris and Philips Gibbon, of four hundred and fifty pounds each at an interest rate of 3% per annum. Both gentlemen were town MPs and had to wait until 1754 for repayment of the debt. The Duke of Newcastle on behalf of the town then repaid the outstanding liability.

The present Town Hall was built and designed by London mason Andrew Jelf in 1742 when the mayor was James Lamb. Rye Town Council still uses the hall today for its regular meetings and it is the third court and market house on this site.

The current building is a two storey and attic fine red brick with Portland stone dressing, and a panelled courtroom. It had traditional open arcading on the ground floor. At the top, a parapet and a cupola are in the centre of the roof and used to house the Jurats bell. They used the bell to announce council meetings and the Quarter Sessions. In 1981, there was restoration on the bell in celebration of the wedding of Prince Charles and Lady Diana.

The ground floor, originally used for a market is fifty-four feet long and twenty-four feet wide and has five massive stone arches supporting the first floor. The building has a main hall some thirty-eight feet long and eighteen feet wide. Upstairs on the second floor is where the town's records were kept. There were also further offices. After the formation of the local fire brigade in 1867, they housed their equipment in the Town Hall from 1870 until 1937. Later the brigade moved to Ferry Road.

On the 12 October 1951, the building gained Grade II status.

Rye Rural District Council was formed in 1894 with K. Reeve elected as the first chairman. They continued in office until the reforms of 1934 and then merged with the new Battle Rural District Council.

In 1894 - 1934, they were meeting in the boardroom of Rye Union, Rye Hill. S.O. Foden with H.W. Parker designed and erected the building in 1843. With the reforms in 1974 and the creating of the Rye Town Council, Rye ceased to be Borough Council.

Rother District Council based in Bexhill Town Hall now governs the town, taking on most of the major duties of the previous Council. The top tier of government is the East Sussex County Council that is situated in Lewes.

Seaford

Seaford formerly Sae-Fiord and in 1058 known as Sefordt in the Rape of Pevensey and Hundred of Flexborough was an old Roman station. Later the town was a Cinque Port partnered with Hastings. With good harbour trading with the continent, the town was thriving, importing wine, wool and corn being the main export in the thirteenth century. The harbour soon disappeared due to movement of the shingle bank. This was caused by the river Ouse breaking a bank and making a new mouth to the sea after a big storm in 1579.

During the Napoleonic Wars (1793–1815), the town became the home of the Martello Tower numbered 74, the most westerly sited defence. Construction started in 1806 and completed by 1810. The cost of works came to eighteen thousand pounds. After many owners, in 1979, the Seaford Museum occupied the building and remains there.

Although this seems a small sleepy seaside town, Henry VIII granted a Charter of Incorporation in August 1544 that brought about the first Local Government. A Municipal Corporation of freemen, Jurats, and bailiff managed the town's needs. The first bailiff elected was John Ockenden in 1541 and the council met at the Town Hall.

For a small-town, it has produced three Prime Ministers namely Henry Pelham (1717 – 1722), William Pitt the Elder (1766 – 1768) and George Canning in 1827.

A railway extension from Newhaven opened in June 1864. Originally, there were plans to lengthen the rail line to Eastbourne but this has never happened. The council has not had a designated Town Hall since moving from the South Street building in 1895.

The municipal building in South Street was a sixteenth-century, one storey, Town Hall with a jail in the basement. The Town Hall was small with a seven-step outside staircase leading up to the entrance door. Inside was a small hallway, before entering the council and court chamber. On the top of the building were a small spire and hipped old tiled roof. The entrance door and windows occupy all the space available in the outer wall, and at the end of the room a small dais with a fixed chair for the bailiff.

The Old Town Hall, South Street, Seaford, East Sussex. BN25 1HP

Along both sides of the wall and up each end of the platform, there was a narrow bench. This was for the bailiff and his associates, the Jurats, under the old corporate regime. In addition, there was a small yard for prisoners to exercise but this has now gone.

After 1886 and the ending of the corporation, the Local Board set up in 1883 used the building. In the 1930s, there was remedial work carried out on the building. They dismantled the old entrance and filled in the underground cells, with a new floor installed at ground level. On the 15 November 1976, the hall achieved Grade II listed status. Later the building suffered severe damaged after a terrible fire in June 1989.

The old Town Hall building is in use today, but not for council business. A Community Organisations Information Centre now occupies the hall. This is the only building in Seaford known officially as the Town Hall although occasionally Hurdis House carried the title.

In July 1883, a Local Board (1883–1894) replaced the previous Corporation who then held their first elections in September of that year.

After the formation of the Seaford Urban District Council in 1894 that was in power until 1974, they merged with Lewes Borough, Newhaven Urban District Council and Chailey Rural District Council. They then became the Lewes District Council.

This state remained until April 1999 when the Parish Council of Seaford was set up. At their meeting the next month, they passed a resolution to change the status of the Council from Parish to Town. This then created the Seaford Town Council in May 1999. The first mayor elected was Laurie Holland. There are now three tiers of local government: Seaford Town Council, Lewes District Council and East Sussex County Council.

3, Clinton Place, Seaford, East Sussex.

On the formation of the Seaford Urban District Council, they held their first meeting in 1895 at No.3, Clinton Place.

The consensus had been that the old Town Hall was too small for the town's needs. Clinton Place was a row of nineteenth-century terraced buildings built about 1870. They were designed with fine iron railing balconies set across the front at the first-floor level. From here on the 28 January 1901, the council read out the proclamation of the Accession of Edward VII. Large crowds attended this event. With the production of many postcards to commemorate the day, this was a memorable occasion for the town. With the town expanding the council were also using other offices for their administration. The council stayed in the building until 1928.

27, Broad Street, Seaford, East Sussex,

The Council moved into the building from Clinton Place and stayed from 1929 until 1931. The town had continuously been growing since 1500 but by the 1931 census, the population had started to shrink. Office space must have been a problem as in 1930 the council started to look for larger premises to carry out business. After the council vacated the building it became the main post office in Seaford. They stayed until their move to Church Street in the 1970s.

Seaford

The Crouch, Bramber Lane, Seaford, East Sussex.

In July 1930, Seaford Urban District Council bought the Crouch House, an early eighteenth-century building and lands, in an auction for four thousand three hundred pounds. The first meeting of the council in their new home was on the 3 June 1931. During WWII, the house was designated an ARP warden control point.

At the entrance to the Crouch Gardens, the council erected a c16 stone archway in 1931. This originally was part of the Town Hall and Courthouse in South Street and discovered when that building was undergoing repairs.

They occupied these premises until March 1966. Later in 1967, the council demolished the building.

After several years derelict, the Lewes District Council, who inherited the land from the old Seaford Urban District Council in 1974, built sheltered accommodation for the elderly. The new building known as Coldstream House opened on 30 January 1975. In 2007, the land returned to the Seaford Town Council authority.

The Downs, Sutton Road, Seaford, East Sussex.

The Downs School founded in 1901 moved to Sutton Road in 1904 and stayed until they closed in 1964. Later the Seaford Urban District Council purchased its lands and buildings in early 1966. They used the grounds of the old school for recreational purposes and the house for council offices with a Council Chamber. Lewes District Council later purchased the building and had their local offices in the building in 1977.

The Lewes council vacated the building in July 1983 and moved their offices back to Lewes. Seaford Town Council also held many of their meetings in the building. Some council departments continued to use the Downs Leisure Centre after the purchase of Hurdis House in 2001.

Hurdis House, 10 Broad Street, Seaford, East Sussex. BN25 1ND

Seaford Town Council purchased the building in early 2001 and named it after the local poet James Hurdis (1763–1801). Born in Bishopstone, he became a clergyman and later in 1793 appointed Professor of Poetry at Oxford University. In 1825, the original house was demolished and then rebuilt about 1865. Buckmaster Joseph Tuck, a surgeon and the last bailiff of Seaford, lived in the house, as well as his executors, in 1911. The Fitzgerald Charity, the leasehold owners sold the building for five hundred and fifty pounds in 1925. Later the National Provincial Bank leased the property until 1947 when they bought the building for fifteen hundred pounds.

The council spent a total of two hundred and seventy-six thousand pounds including repairs and refurbishment of this nineteenth century ordinary building.

Lord Lieutenant of East Sussex, Phyllida Stewart-Roberts, on the 31 May 2001, officially opened the new 'Town Hall'.

Unfortunately, the building did not accommodate the full council or the planning and highways committee, both of which continued to meet at the Downs Leisure Centre. The council stayed here until December 2007 when they moved to Church Street.

37 Church Street, Seaford, East Sussex, BN25 1HG

The Council moved into Church Street in January 2008 after three years of discussion and possibly created a precedent, as this is the police building. Seaford's new Police Station built-in 1969 has let offices to the Citizen Advice Bureau, Tourist Information, Lewes District Council, East Sussex County Council and the Seaford Town Council. The building is a typical red brick, flat roofed, two-storey plain 1960s mundane structure.

It was usual for Town Halls to include a Police or Fire station, but this must be a first for the Police Station to include the Town Council offices.

Winchelsea

Sussex coastal towns have suffered greatly from storms and coastal erosion over the years, with ports and rivers, silting up. No town experienced this more than Winchelsea. The town was originally by the coast on a flat shingle island at the mouth of the river Rother near Rye and in the Rape of Hastings and the Hundred of Guestling. In its heyday, town and port were more important than Rye. In ancient times, the town was called 'Vincenesium' and with a Saxon name of 'Gwent-chesel-ey', (the shingle isle on the level). A Cinque Port (1191) the town used to be by the East side of the river Rother near to Camber.

The unusually bad storms in October 1250 severely damaged three hundred houses, bridges, mills and some churches. This led to a visit on the 2 July 1276 by King Edward I. He arranged to draw up plans to transfer the town to a safer site on higher ground and donated land. Work began on erecting the new town of Winchelsea with the Warden of the Cinque Ports, and the mayor of London, Henry de Waleys.

Unfortunately the great storm of the 5 February 1287 saw the destruction of the old town of Winchelsea. In April 1288, the new town officially opened. The plans for the town were set out on a grid and as was customary in the old town bailiffs governed it. The new town without its port was never as successful and the original proposals for the town were never fully completed.

The town is a corporation by prescription and has never received a charter. Bailiffs and corporate officers governed the town until the town elected a mayor. The first recorded mayor in 1295 was Gervase Alard junior. Winchelsea is believed to be one of the smallest towns in the country to have its own mayor and corporation. A mayor elected on Easter Monday and twelve Jurats governs the town today. It lost its civic and judicial powers in 1886 after the 1883 Municipal Corporation Act. After the Divided Parishes Act 1882 the town is in the parish of Icklesham and falls under the governance of the Rother District Council.

Common to many towns along the South coast, Winchelsea suffered badly from attacks by the French in 1360 and the Spanish in 1380. Most public buildings and the original Town Hall suffered severely from fire damage.

9, High Street, Winchelsea, East Sussex. TN36 4EA

The old records state that by the end of the fifteenth century, **'the last merchant had left the town'** and there was no longer a port.

By 1538, work began on the construction of Winchelsea Castle with completion by 1544. The cost for works was twenty-three thousand pounds. Since the eighteenth century, the name of the castle has been Camber Castle.

The present Town Hall and Court House is a late thirteenth-century building and it is interesting as the only specimen of medieval municipal architecture in Sussex. There were major restorations of the building in both the fifteenth and sixteenth centuries. These included extensions to the North and East of the hall.

During the late eighteenth century, the court moved to the upper floor and the lower floor of the building became the Town gaol until 1879. From 1557, the building was used as a Town Hall, and still is in use today by the mayor of the town for ceremonial affairs.

Dr. Edwin Freshfield had given the building to the town in 1890, as the council had only been tenants. It is now in a trust for all the town's residents. The town's museum situated on the first floor opened in 1950 with the building granted Grade I status on the 3 August 1961.

A two-storey building built of rubble stone, a stone doorway, cellar and tiled gable ended roof.

There is heavy timbering to the ceilings of the lower and open roof of the upper chambers. Both of these chambers, with modern windows, have large fireplaces with flat segmental arches supported by plain shafts and corbels. The building originally built for Gervase Alard junior as a private house that had an extension built. Originally, called the Freemans Hall this later changed to the Court Hall. The North and East extensions were demolished and removed in 1666.

In 2002, there was work on the Court Hall when the roof was retiled.

The railway station some 1km from the town opened in February 1851 and still operates today although there is only a limited service available.

Now we are in the twenty-first century it is surprising for such an old town there has never been a female mayor elected. The town has for many years petitioned to become a civil parish in its own right. This matter is still being debated.

7 Miscellaneous East Sussex.

The local government of a town uses a building for the town or civic business, and these are not always purpose built buildings. Some towns have had Town Halls in the past. Now some of these have gone, due to various reasons. Sometimes small towns and parishes take over an existing building for their meetings. A town with a town council and a mayor using a specific building regularly for municipal meetings should rightly call that building the Town Hall.

In the East Sussex County, there are ten Town Councils, one City Council and eighty-two Parish Councils although not all parishes have councils. These are located in Lewes, Rother and Wealden. There are not any parish councils in Eastbourne and Hastings and no town council in Bexhill. Brighton and Hove are now a city.

The Town Councils are... Lewes Town Council, Battle, Newhaven, Rye, Peacehaven, Crowborough, Seaford, Hailsham, Telscombe, Uckfield. Some of the services offered by these councils are, allotments, cemeteries, parish lighting, bus shelters, litterbins, playgrounds and recreation grounds

Battle

A market town in the Rape of Hastings and Hundred of Battle, and originally known as Epyton or Epiton 'heath land'. After the Battle of Hastings in October 1066, William Duke of Normandy built an abbey in the town. This was at the request of the Pope, in penance for the loss of life in the battle. Henry 1 (1068 - 1135) granted the town a Market Charter in 1114. In about 1400 by the Abbey stood a grand gatehouse with a large tower with arches and columns. The town was recognised as a significant manufacturer of fine gunpowder (1676–1847) with the first mill built by John Hammond. This industry supplied the British army right up to the Crimean War and considered the best in Europe.

The town's governing council used the Old Abbey Gate House as the Town Hall and Court House until 1794 when the roof collapsed and it became unfit for use. Due to neglect, the interior of the building fell into ruin although later they rebuilt it. A local account at the time states;

" Thursday se'nnight, part of the roof of Battle Abbey, Sussex, which, by permission, has been used as a town-hall, was, by the vigilance of the wind and rain, drove in. This totally destroyed that part of the noble building, and put the inhabitants of the town in the greatest consternation; some thinking it a dreadful clap of thunder, others that it was an earthquake."
1794

The railway arrived in Battle in early 1852. The station designed by William Tress, the South Eastern Railway architect, is a fine example of Gothic style. It is now a Grade II listed building.

A Local Board governed the town from 1851 until 1894, meeting at the boardroom of the Union Workhouse. They later met at The George Hotel in 1882 until the reforms of 1894 and the forming of the Battle Urban District Council (1894 – 1934).

The Urban District Council also met at the Council room in the George Hotel between the years 1894 - 1922. The first chairman of the council was W.A. Raper. In 1923 and 1924, meetings of the Urban Council were at the Star Hotel and at 6 High Street from 1925 until 1934.

They governed the town until the Local Government reforms of 1934 when the enlarged Battle Rural District Council (1934 – 1974) succeeded them.

Battle Rural District Council (1894 – 1934), whose first chairman was Rev T.W. Adams met at the Poor Law Institute between 1894 and 1934. This 1840 building cost seven thousand three hundred pounds and was designed by Frederick Thatcher, a locally born architect.

The new enlarged Battle Rural District Council of 1934 met at 11 Wellington Square in Hastings and then by 1938 had offices at the old coach house at Watch Oak, Battle. The Rural District Council later bought the building and built a new wing containing a council chamber on the ground floor and offices above. Their first chairman was C.J. Honisett who had also been chairman of the old Rural District Council.

The Battle Parish Council held their first meeting on 12 April 1934 at the Church Hall with chairman Cllr Fovargue. Later they were at 6 High Street until they moved to the Almonry. In May 1934, the parish council agreed to take over the responsibility for the upkeep and insurance of the town's fire engine.

With the Local Government Act 1972, Battle Rural District Council merged with Rye Borough Council and Bexhill Borough Council to form the new Rother District Council in April 1974. The new Rother District Council's main offices are now at Bexhill Town Hall.

Battle Town Council formed in 1974 and now has its offices at The Almonry in the High Street. G.H. Cramp became the first chairman. He had held that post in the old Parish Council. It was after an election in 1987 that the status of a mayor of Battle came about. Cllr Robert Emeleus was the first to hold this position.

The Almonry building in the past was leased to various individuals until in the early 1980s the Council took up the tenancy. This building had never been an Almonry. Although rumoured to stand on the grounds of a former Almonry of 1090. Known in the early Middle Ages as 'Knight's' and named after an important local landowner family. The old records show the property was part of the Abbey Estate and had a number of tenants until it reverted to the Abbey in 1800.

The Almonry, High Street, Battle, East Sussex TN33 0EA

In about 1930, the owners sold the building. It stayed in private ownership until the early 1980s when the County Council acquired the tenancy. Later in 1987, the Town Council bought the site that now includes the Town Museum, a public garden and the Town Council offices.

The building is an example of an oak framed timber house with a hipped old tiled roof. It was originally a five bay hall house built in the fifteenth century. There have been changes over the years with some parts demolished, others parts rebuilt. An extension and installation of chimneys, as well as other changes, took place in the sixteenth century when the house was converted to form a courtyard town house.

There were further works in the seventeenth and twentieth centuries with renovations in sandstone to the ground floor. In addition, on the first floor, they hung red tiles on the exterior wall.

The Grade II Almonry building became a listed structure on the 3 August 1961.

Crowborough

Crowborough, previously in the Rape of Pevensey and Hundred of Rotherfield, is the largest and highest inland town in East Sussex. The town borders the Ashdown Forest at eight hundred feet above sea level and used to promote itself as 'Scotland in Sussex'. There have been many names for the village from the early days and has been known as Crotesberghe, Crottesburge, Crowbergh. Since the seventeenth century, the town has used the name Crowborough.

The railway station opened in August 1868 and originally called Rotherfield. Afterwards in 1880, the rail station changed its name and they adopted the town name Crowborough. Again, in 1897, the name changed to Crowborough and Jarvis Brook, until May 1980 when it reverted to Crowborough.

A golf course opened in 1895 and in 1904 the fire station, with a horse-drawn steam fire appliance, opened on the High Street.

There had been a Volunteer Fire Brigade in the town since February 1900 following the destruction of Walsh Manor the previous year. The Uckfield Fire Service had attended this.

In September 1880, Crowborough achieved local autonomy forming an ecclesiastical parish. They had previously been part of Rotherfield Parish.

Crowborough Parish Council was set up on the 6 April 1905. They elected John Booker as their first chairman, a position he held until 1932. Offices for the council were at the Wolfe Recreation Ground, Blackness Road. These grounds were gifted to the town by Miss Wolfe, who was a descendant of General James Wolfe (1727 – 1759), who was known for his victory at the Battle of Quebec.

In 1905, the Parish Council started a campaign that lasted many years trying to gain Urban Council status. Unfortunately, the town never achieved these plans and it was not until 1988 that the town gained Town Council recognition.

On the 22 December 1987, the Parish Council bought the Library building in the Broadway from East Sussex County Council for one hundred and twenty thousand pounds. The building, now the Town Hall, still houses the council.

The Broadway, Crowborough,
East Sussex. TN6 1DA

The Town Council came into being on 24 May 1988 after many years trying to gain Town Council status. The first elected mayor was Paul D Scott, who was also the last chairman of the Parish Council.

Crowborough Town Council over the last few years considered purchasing the Pine Grove building, home of Wealden District Council. In February 2015, the council agreed to go ahead with this. The guide price for the sale of the building was £1.7m. By July 2015, this matter remains unresolved.

The Duchess of Gloucester opened a new community centre on the 18 April 2012 behind the Pine Grove office block. The building costs were £3m. The Crowborough Community Centre has leased the offices on a 125-year lease for a nominal amount of £1 a year. The building contains the main hall and three meeting rooms for hire, as well as a café and free Wi-Fi.

Wealden District Council

Pine Grove, Crowborough, East Sussex. TN6 1DH

After the reorganisations and establishment of the Wealden District Council in 1973 – 1974 from the Hailsham and Uckfield Rural District Councils, they met first in Starfield in Beacon Road. Subsequently in the years 1986 - 1988, they built a new office in Pine Grove, Crowborough. The first meeting in the building was in February 1988. Hubbard Ford Partnership of Hove designed the new office block with the Council's own in-house team designing the interior.

The ground floor occupied by the council and officially opened on 14 April 1988 by the Lord Lieutenant of East Sussex, the Marquess of Abergavenny KG OBE. On the first floor was the new library, which Cllr Mrs Arlene Rowe, the Chair of East Sussex County Council Libraries and Records Committee, opened on the 30 June 1988. The costs of the new building were about £2.9m funded by the sale of other council properties vacated.

The first chairman of the council was Mr H.R. Searle, elected to office in 1973. Later still in 2012 they moved most of their key offices to larger premises in Vicarage Lane, Hailsham. The new building in Hailsham completed on time by Willmott Dixon Construction was within the set budget. The total cost of moving the council offices and staff was £6.5m.

Hailsham

The market town of Hailsham first settled in 490 A.D. and in the Rape of Pevensey and Hundred of Dill. The Domesday Book of 1086 records the village called 'Hamelesham'. Henry III granted the village a Market Charter in 1252. This market continued until the seventeenth century and later was reinstated in 1786. Known as 'Aylesham' in the thirteenth century and not until the late 1600s was the name Hailsham adopted. The village has a long history of agriculture and industry.

Over time, the village expanded with many trades started by local men. The village renowned for tanning and leatherwork as well, from 1807, its rope making started by Thomas Burfield (1785 - 1866). By the mid - nineteenth century, it held the largest cattle market in Sussex.

There were large military barracks erected on Hailsham Common in 1803 that housed up to one thousand men and closed in 1815 after the defeat of Napoleon at Waterloo.

In the early years, the Vestry held their meetings in many different places in the town. Premises used were the South chapel of St Mary's church, the Kings Head at Cacklebury, the Crown Inn and George Inn. As well as the Terminus Hotel and Infants' school, until the building of the new Vestry Room above the fire station in 1889.

The 14 May 1849 saw the arrival of a railway link from Polegate and by 1880 there was a rail extension connecting the town to Heathfield. This service also connected to Tunbridge Wells. The rail line locally named the 'Cuckoo Line' closed in 1965, with the Polegate section closing in 1968.

The Hailsham Parish Council had managed the town after the first parish council elections and their initial meeting of 3 January 1895. The first chairman to be elected was the Rev Francis Clyde Harvey, who held that position until 1919. The Council held its meetings between 1899 and 1930 in the boardroom of the Workhouse built in 1836 in Union Road. Over time, the name of the road has changed to Hawks Road.

The Rural District Council set up in 1895 after the reforms of the previous year elected J.W.M. Ashley as chairman at their first meeting in January.

Hailsham

They met at the Union buildings between the years 1895 and 1930 in Union Road, now Hawks Road. H.R. Searle was the last chairman of the council in 1973.

Under the reforms of the Local Government Act of 1972 saw the creation of the Wealden District Council in April 1974. This new council, made up from the merger of the old Hailsham and Uckfield Rural District Councils now has its headquarters in Hailsham. On the 20 May 1973 Hailsham Parish Council elected to have its own Town Council and on the 20 May 1974, the new council came into being.

17, London Road, Hailsham, East Sussex.

Hailsham Rural District Council had offices in the building from 1904 until 1933 when they moved into Cortlandt House.

Cortlandt House, George Street, Hailsham, East Sussex. BN27 1AE

Cortlandt House is a late eighteenth-century Georgian building (1793) on two storeys and an attic with a tiled roof.

There are three bays on the ground and first floor with red brick quoins. In 1881, there were additions to the end of the building adding four-sided bays. On the 30 August 1966, the building received Grade II listing status.

At first, the name of the building was 'Newhouse'. Its original owner John Bristow was the owner of this and the surrounding paddock. On his death in 1803 he bequeathed it to his daughter Mrs Mary Sly (nee Bristow). The house was sold in 1881 and the new owner, William Strickland JP (1836 - 1918), renamed it after Colonel Philip van Cortlandt (New York, November 1739 – Hailsham, May 1814). The American Royalist stationed in Hailsham rented the house from Mrs Slye the daughter of John Bristow in 1803. He should not be confused with his cousin Brigadier Colonel Philip van Cortlandt (New York September 1749 – November 1831) the American patriot.

After Colonel Van Cortlandt died the Slye family (Marthanna Bristow) and then T. Falkner occupied 'Newhouse' before William Strickland acquired the building in 1881.

Hailsham Rural District Council purchased the building in 1932 at auction after the death of Mrs Strickland for two thousand five hundred pounds. They moved their offices into the building in 1933 and stayed until 1982 and the setting up of the new Wealden District Council. Hailsham Council sold the building in 1982. The newly formed Wealden District Council also had offices in the building from 1974 until their move to new offices in Vicarage Lane in 1982.

'Cortlandt' has had a chequered history since. In 1985, Real Land Limited bought the building then later in March 2003, Personal Travel Service took possession of the house. They renovated the outside and interior. In 2008, Cortlandt Property LLP acquired the building for four hundred and seventy thousand pounds. There were further repairs and now houses several private small businesses.

After a fire next door in Downford House built by Mr H.C. Sinnock in 1838, the Town Council moved to the Inglenook in Market Street. The parish council had also held meetings in the building.

Hailsham

The Inglenook, Market St, Hailsham, East Sussex, BN27 2AE

The Parish Council elected to adopt town status on the 25 May 1973. The new Hailsham Town Council voted T. Jeffrey Holman as their first mayor. He had been previously the chairman of the late Parish Council. In the early 1980s, the Council moved to the Inglenook but in 1984, they moved offices to the newly built community hall. In 1987, the council moved back into the building and the mayor, Ron Harmer, officially opened the new 'Town Hall' in December 1987. The mayor of Uckfield, Peter Cameron-Waller, and Wealden District Council's deputy chairman, also attended.

This building used to be the Fleur-de-Lys Inn built in 1542 on Horseye Road, later known as Market Street. The Inglenook and the Fleur-de-Lys were originally one large gable-ended building. In 1762, the Parish Council bought the Inn and used it as the Parish Workhouse until 1854. An auctioneer's clerk a David Guy on 17 January 1868 then moved into the building.

In the late nineteenth century, it was decided to divide the building into two, creating separate small commercial units. They comprised a carriage works, a bakehouse (in the 1860s), Mr Miller's butchers shop and a Post Office (1871 - 89).

On the 25 September 1889, a fire began in an office above the Wheelwright shop at the rear. This destroyed most of the Eastern side of the building. The Post Office, originally located on the North side of the building, then moved across the road. Following repairs to the building, this later became a private house.

At a Vestry meeting on 25 October, discussions took place about building a fire station and a new Vestry office with the money received from the Royal Exchange Assurance Company. It was not until a meeting on 2 January 1890 when the council reached a consensus. There was an inquiry in May 1890 and Benjamin Stonestreet, a local builder and carpenter, presented his costs for the construction.

The Hailsham Auxiliary Fire service formed in 1877 housed a manual fire engine at the Terminus Hotel and had a loan of two horses when needed. Later in 1893, they sold the engine to the new Herstmonceux fire service for thirty pounds.

Eventually, the council moved in 1890 into their new red brick and slate roofed fire station with the Vestry offices on the first floor, on Market Street. It was the first time the Vestry had their own offices as they had previously met at local schools or inns. The Fire Brigade stayed until their new fire station in Victoria Road opened in 1958.

Later Jehovah's Witnesses used the building and then the Town Council, until their move to Vicarage Lane in 1982. Its use was afterwards a bakery, an antique shop and now trades as a takeaway kebab shop.

The Blackman family took over the rest of the building in 1892 and started repairs in 1893. The building was timber-framed with tiled roof and casement windows and ground floor with a modern portion at the South end. The Blackmans stayed through generations until Frederick Blackman died in March 1963.

The building remained in private hands until the Town Council moved back in 1987 where they still are today. It received Grade II status on the 13 October 1952.

Wealden District Council

Council Offices, Vicarage Lane, Hailsham,
East Sussex, BN27 2AX

Under the reforms of the Local Government Act 1972, April 1974 saw the creation of Wealden District Council. This council is a merger of the old Hailsham and Uckfield Rural District Councils. The council holds elections every four years and now there are fifty-five councillors.

There are thirty-five Parish Councils, four Town Councils (Crowborough, Hailsham, Polegate and Uckfield) and two Parish Meetings within the authority of Wealden Council.

Hailsham is now the home of Wealden District Council, the second tier of local government. They have their own nine hundred thousand pounds, fine modern 1981 – 1982, red brick buildings in Vicarage Lane. The council staff moved in March 1982.

They previously had offices in Cortlandt House, as well as in Prospect House in Victoria Road, Hailsham and Polegate. Prior to this, the council held full meetings at Starfield in Crowborough until the move to Pine Grove, Crowborough and subsequent move to Hailsham. The first chairman of the council was Mr H.R. Searle elected to office in 1973. In 2005, there was refurbishment work to the Vicarage Lane offices for a new reception area that opened to the public on 1 August 2005.

Again, in 2011 - 2012, there were refurbishments and an extension to the building by Willmott Dixon Construction and architects Frankham Consultancy Group Ltd. The total costs for works were one hundred and eighty-eight thousand pounds and the building reopened to the public on 6 August 2012.

Pine Grove council offices in Crowborough are now empty awaiting forthcoming plans about its future.

Newhaven

Newhaven anciently known as Meeching by the Saxons is on the banks at the mouth of the River Ouse. It was in the Rape of Lewes and the Hundred of Holmestrow. The town's name changed after the great storm of 1579 when New Haven succeeded Seaford as the main port for goods and exports for Lewes. After the wreck of the H.M.S Brazen in 1800, the local people with the help of Lloyds of London funded one of the first lifeboats in the United Kingdom in May 1803. This incident occurred just West of Newhaven port.

The lifeboat a Greathead 'Original' design had ten oars and a crew of thirteen. Later they sent the boat to Brighton, as it was heavy and unpopular with the local crews. This was twenty-one years before the foundation of the RNLI. Newhaven has always been an important port and a possible target for invaders. Since the Bronze Age, there has been a fort to protect the town.

The current fort had forty-two guns and a capacity for three hundred men. Erected between 1864 and 1871, the costs were about one hundred and fifty thousand pounds. Lieutenant John Charles Ardagh of the Royal Engineers was in charge of design and construction.

Newhaven Council bought the Fort in 1962 for thirteen thousand pounds. Although in good condition when purchased, the buildings, disused, fell into disrepair. Lewes District Council inherited the Fort and in 1981 two local developers started working on transforming the buildings. There have been many changes since and in 1988, Lewes District Council reopened the Fort as a military heritage attraction.

The town developed with the coming of the railway in 1847 and set up ferry routes to Caen, St. Nazaire and Jersey (1850 - 63). As well as a service to Dieppe (1853) that previously had left from Brighthelmstone (Brighton). By 1882, the port of Newhaven was importing timber, slates, granite and farm products and it continued to expand.

During the First World War, it was a major port for movement of men and equipment. Again, in World War 2, it was the departure point for Canadian troops in 1942 on their way to Dieppe.

Newhaven Local Board (1881 – 1894) meeting in the High Street, with George Stone their first chairman, governed the town. Then the reforms of the Local Government Act 1894 saw the formation of the Newhaven Urban District Council (1894 – 1974). They held their meetings first at 8 High Street (1894 - 1902) then at 34 Meeching Road (1903-07) and later at the new building in 20 Fort Road.

20, Fort Road, Newhaven, East Sussex BN9 9QF

The Town Hall was built and erected in 1906 by Charles Cooke of Brighton Road with architect Frederick J. Rayner, the council surveyor. The chairman, councillor F. Baldwin JP officially opened the building. It now houses offices of the Lewes District Council.

The Fire Brigade used to keep a fire engine, tender and fire escape ladder at the council offices in Fort Road.

This was from 1907 until the late 1940s and their move back to Meeching Road in the town.

After the reforms in 1974, the Newhaven Town Council held their meetings at 18 Fort Road. They appointed C.A.M. Campbell as the first mayor and still use the building for the town's affairs. Nowadays Lewes District Council carries out most services, but the town still has a mayor and Newhaven Town Council hold public meetings in various places around the town.

18, Fort Road, Newhaven, East Sussex BN9 9QF

Plans were made in July 2014 to build a new fire station in Meeching Road on the Saxonholme site and next door to the old fire station vacated in 1966. This would also incorporate the police station and Lewes District Council offices. Morgan Sindall plc. of Brighton were contracted to construct the new headquarters. Work started in October 2014 on the new building called Saxon House that will also house a drill yard and tower.

The building was completed 22 January 2016 and a handing over ceremony took place on 7 December 2015. The official opening will be later in the 2016.

The Newhaven Rural District Council, formed in 1894, held all of its meetings in the Workhouse and Poor Law Institute, Church Hill. Sampson Kempthorne designed the Institute building at a cost of three thousand three hundred pounds in 1835. The council ceased business in March 1934.

Peacehaven

Community House, Meridan Centre,
Meridian Way, Peacehaven, East Sussex BN10 8BB

The town has Charles William Neville, born Charles William Neville Ussher (1881 – 1960), to thank for its existence. An Englishman born in Darlington, County Durham, he emigrated at a young age with his parents to Canada and attended the university in Toronto. Later he moved to Australia. After amassing his fortune in New Guinea, he then returned to Canada and after a while moved back to England.

On his arrival in England, he bought six hundred acres of lands in the parishes of Piddinghoe and Telscombe in Sussex in 1914.

Originally, he named the new town New Anzac-on-Sea after an advertised competition in the Times and other national newspapers.

There had been a prize offered for a new name for the town of a plot of land worth one hundred pounds. Mr C West of Ilford and Mr Kemp of Maidstone, Kent won it. The name of the town changed in 1917 to Peacehaven and the village started to grow slowly. The dreams of its founder never came to anything and now there is just a small sprawl of a town.

Peacehaven came under the governance of Newhaven District Council and then later in 1934 the Chailey Rural District Council.

The Peacehaven Parish Council was formed in 1929. Following the reorganisation of Local Government in 1974, they changed to the Peacehaven Town Council. The new council held their meetings in Phyllis Avenue until the move to the Meridian Centre. Nineteen seventy-nine saw the election of the town's first mayor, Cllr Anthony S Payne.

East Sussex County Council filed planning application on land that they owned for a Supermarket, shops, flats and a community centre and approval came on the 22 May 1977. Kier Ltd of Lewes built the Meridian Centre and it opened in April 1979. Michael Shanks of the National Consumer Council opened the Council offices on the 23 April 1979. The Mall has various shops and other services, including the Town Council Offices, Social Services, a Library and a large supermarket.

The council remained the administrative owner until 31 March 1988 when Rugby Securities Holdings Ltd took over. The owners changed again and in 2003, The Co-operative Estates Company took over management of the Centre. Now under a new administration, there were major improvements to the buildings in 2004 to comply with the Disability Discrimination Act. More refurbishment took place in 2010 and works completed in December 2014.

Polegate

The small settlement previously known as 'Powlegate Corner' according to records of 1563 and later by 1569 known as 'Poolgate'. The name changed in the mid-nineteenth century with the arrival of the railways in 1846 and the start of the development of the town.

Farming, brick, and tile making were the main industries.

Polegate

In the early days, the trains terminated in Polegate. There was a freight terminal, and this helped the town to expand and prosper. Passengers for Eastbourne and Hailsham had to alight and travel by coach and horse to conclude their journeys. It was after 1849, with a rail extension to Eastbourne and Hailsham that passengers could travel directly to the coast or to the market of Hailsham.

49, High Street, Polegate, East Sussex BN26 6AL

During World War 1, the town was first in the Dover command and then home for the Portsmouth Command and had a one hundred and forty-two-acre site for the airship station, Polegate RNAS. The site was selected in 1914 and work started on the construction in early 1915.

The base commissioning was on the 6 July 1915, but by February 1920, the air base had ceased to operate. The airships used to patrol the English Channel looking for enemy submarines or ships. In early 1915 saw the stationing of the first airship, a type S.S in Polegate when Lieutenant Lock was the base commanding officer. The airfield was on land south of the Polegate-Willingdon Road in Willingdon and spread through to Wannock. It was named after the nearest railway station, which of course was Polegate. In December 1916, Mr Asquith the Prime Minister visited the base.

In the early years, the small village was part of the Hailsham parish. Polegate was part of the Hailsham Rural Council from 1940 until 1973 and the reforms of 1972. In 1974, with the creation of the Wealden District Council, the Parish Council came under their control. Polegate Town Council came into being in July 1985 meeting monthly in the Council Chamber in the High Street. The town now has its own mayor. In 1992, the first elected mayor of Polegate was Councillor Ian Tankard. The elections for councillors are held every four years. Wannock Recreation Centre held previous meetings of the Parish Council, as well as the council, utilising a school in Polegate and offices in the High Street. The 'Town Hall' in the High Street used to be a builders merchant business, which had traded in the town for many years. In October 2000, the council moved into the building giving them a permanent home.

There are three tiers of government; the Town Council then Wealden District Council and the East Sussex County Council serving the town. For national representation, Polegate is in the Lewes Parliamentary Constituency

Telscombe

Telscombe Civic Centre, 360 South Coast Road,
Telscombe Cliffs, East Sussex. BN10 7ES

Telscombe

The village originally in the Rape of Lewes and the Hundred of Holstrow can trace records of the manor back to the time of King Edgar. In Saxon times, the village name was Titelescumbe. The manor has changed hands many times over the years. In 1900, James Ambrose Harman became Lord of the Manor and later on 1 September 1924, Charles William Neville, the man responsible for the expansion of Peacehaven acquired the title.

Ambrose Gorham (October 1853 – June 1933) who moved to Telscombe in 1893, owned most of the village of Telscombe. He had wanted to become the Lord of the Manor but was thwarted in his plans by Mr Neville. Gorham was a bookmaker and horse trainer. After his horse, Shannon Lass won the Grand National in 1902, at his own expense, supplied electricity in 1930, and mains water supplies in July 1909 to all the flint walled houses in the village. He also arranged the restoration of the interior of the tenth-century church. This made Telscombe the first all-electric village in the country. In 1924, he built a clubhouse for his local stable lads and this later became the village hall. After his death, he bequeathed most of the village to a trust known as 'Gorham's Gift' to Brighton Corporation on condition the area 'is preserved for the people of the area'.

The Parish Council (1929 – 1974) was first formed in January 1929 and held their meetings in the Parish Hall, Tyedean Road with Major C.H. Cooper as chairman. With the changes in Local Government in 1974 and the increase in population, the council elected to become a Town Council with an elected mayor. Mrs Molly E Pratten held this position. The Town Council held their meetings at the Parish Hall until the building of the new Civic Centre in 2001. Telscombe Tye, Telscombe Cliffs and Telscombe Village all are part Telscombe Town Council. The Town Council purchased a plot of land on the South Coast Road, in April 1997 and applied for planning permission in February 1998 for a new Civic Centre. With the help of the Public Works Loan Board, the council secured a loan of two hundred thousand pounds towards the cost of the new centre. They chose to appoint architects Brian Sellars Associates of Lewes for the works. The Town Clerk occupied some ground floor offices in February 2000 with the building works completed in 2001. The new Civic Centre stands on land that once housed the South Coast Land and Resort Company.

Uckfield

The village previously known in ancient times as 'Ockfelde' or variations of the name, but is without a mention in the Domesday record.

The first records of the town were in 1220 when the town known as 'Uckefeld' held a weekly market. There was cloth making as well as a pottery industry and in 1574, ironworks. The town recorded in the Rape of Pevensey and the Hundred of Loxfield Dorset and from 14 April 1859 governed by a Local Board.

Uckfield was the main stopping point for pilgrims on the journey from Canterbury to Lewes and Chichester. The railway first came to the town with the Lewes and Uckfield Railway in October 1858 with connections from Lewes to Brighton and Eastbourne. The rail line to Lewes has since closed. The old rail station was in use up to 1991 when a new station replaced it.

The Board holding meeting in 1882 at the Workhouse and then at the Maiden's Head Hotel (1887 – 94), now a listed building in the High Street until the reforms of 1894. After this date, the Urban District Council (February 1895 – March 1934), made up of fifteen members, took over the governance. They met from 1894 until 1934 in the Public Hall/Town Hall, built-in 1877 on the West side of the High Street.

Robert Wheeler, an architect from Tunbridge Wells, designed this building on land given to the town by R.S. Streatfield. The cost with furnishings was about two thousand pounds.

Originally the Hall had an indented portico and three Gothic arches in stone and coloured brickwork that were supported by two columns with carved capitols. There were two entrances to the building, one on the North side and the other on the East side. The newly formed Public Hall Company raised the money for the building by public subscription. In 1886, they built an extension to house the Conservative Club. Again, in 1907, there were further works to the building. That then changed the character of a fine structure into something very ordinary. Since 1996, it has been the home of the local library.

Uckfield Rural District Council (1894 – 1974) met at the Workhouse designed by H.E. Kendall, between the years 1894 to 1927. This was an 1839 plain brick building at Ringwood that later in 1985 was demolished.

The council then moved to rented offices in Church Street (1928 - 1930). They paid a rent of forty pounds per annum but the building was inadequate for council business. Later in June 1928, the council bought Starfield in Crowborough for their headquarters. The purchase price was three and a half thousand pounds.

Starfield was a house built about 1890 for Dr Isaac Roberts. He was a master builder and prominent amateur astronomer and pioneer of astrophotography.

The council with their chairman, Francis Barchard, held their first meeting in the new home on the 30 September 1930. In 1934, after the staff increased from seventeen to twenty-nine, there were building works and changes, including a new Council Chamber. These cost just over four thousand pounds. October 1935 was the first time the council used the new Council Chamber.

With the new changes in 1934, the Urban District Council merged into the new Uckfield Rural District Council meeting at Council offices, Starfield, Beacon Road, Crowborough until further changes in 1974.

After the government reorganisations of 1974 came the formation of the Uckfield Town Council with the first town mayor being Cllr A. J. Hall. The council used to meet at council offices, then Wealden Lodge (now demolished) in Hempstead Lane from 1986 until 1991 before moving into the new Civic Centre in 1991.

Uckfield Civic Centre, Bell Farm Lane,
Uckfield, East Sussex TN22 1AE

The town mayor, Cllr E.J. Daly, officially opened the new red brick Civic Centre on the 8 September 1991 although the council had moved into the building on 1 July. Its first full Town Council meeting in the building was on the 9 July.

The cost of building the new Civic Centre was raised by public subscription. Many local businesses also supported the funding. There is a board on display in the Centre with the names of companies and private individuals who contributed donations for the Civic Centre. The Centre also houses a restaurant and coffee shop and there are seven function rooms for hire.

With the formation in 1974 of Wealden District Council, made up of the old Uckfield and Hailsham Rural District Councils, they held their meetings in Crowborough. The District Council later moved to purpose-built offices in Hailsham.

Glossary

ARP: ... Air Raid Precautions, set up in U.K. in 1924 to protect civilians.
Attic: ... Small top storey within the roof.

Baluster: ... Small pillar or column of fanciful outline.
Balustrade: ...Series of balusters supporting a handrail.
Bay Window: ...One projecting from the face of a building.

Carillon: ...Set of bells usually hung in a tower.
Coade Stone: ...Artificial cast stone of the c18+c19 by Coade and Sealy of London.
Cupola: ...A small dome used as a crowning feature.

Dado: ...Decorative covering of the lower part of the wall.
Dais: ...Raised platform at one end of a room.
Dormer: ...Window placed vertically in the sloping plane of a roof.

Finial: ...Top of a canopy, gable, pinnacle.

Gables: ...Triangular upper part of a wall between the sloping ends of a pitched roof.
Gothic: ...Style of later Middle Ages characterized by the pointed arch.

Headborough: ...Elected honorary official responsible for maintaining law and order.
Hipped Roof: ...Roof with sloped instead of vertical ends.

Jurat: ... In the old corporations, Jurats are officers who have much the same power as aldermen. They are appointed to assist the mayor with his responsibilities and functions and with him form the Corporation.

Oriel: ...Window projecting above ground level.

Parapet: ...Wall for the protection of a sudden drop.
Pediment: ...A formalized gable also used over doors or windows.
Pilasters: ...Flat representation of a classical column in shallow relief.
Porch: ...Low structure projecting from the doorway of a building and forming a covered entrance.
Portico: ...Centrepiece of a building with detached or attached classical columns and a pediment.

Quoins: ...Dressed stones at the angles of a building.

Rusticate:...Marking masonry with sunken joints or roughened surface.

Stucco: ...Durable lime plaster used as external protective coating.

Turret: ...Very small tower.

Undercroft: ...Vaulted room sometimes underground.

Vestry: ... Parish members meeting for secular and church government business. Name used for the room as well as for the committees.

Bibliography

Antram. N & Morrice.R – 2008 - **Brighton and Hove** – Yale University Press.

Bell.C.R.V. – 1975 - **A History of East Sussex County Council 1889-1974** – Phillimore & Co Ltd.

Black, Adam& Charles - 1861- **S-E Counties of England -Sussex**. – Blacks Guide.

Brent, Colin. – 2004 – **Pre-Georgian & Georgian Lewes** – Colin Brent Books.

Brooker.J. – 1888+1899 - **Guide & Directory for Uckfield and District** – J.Brooker.

Carder, Tim – 1990 – **Encyclopaedia of Brighton**.

Catchpole, J. – 1962 - **The Restoration & Repairs to the front elevation of County Hall, Lewes,**– Sussex Archaeological Society – Vol 100.

Cheal, Henry. – 1921 - **The Story of Shoreham**– Combridge, Hove.

Cooper, William Durrent - 1850 – **The History of Winchelsea** – John Russel Smith, London.

Cousins, Henry – 1920 – **Hastings of Bygone Days** – and the present – F.J.Parsons Ltd. Hastings.

Dallaway, James. – 1815 - **History of Western Division of County of Sussex** –
T.Bensley.

Dale, Antony. – 1950 - **History & Architecture of Brighton** – Bredon & Heginbothom Ltd.

Dally, Richard. – 1831 - **The Chichester Guide** – P.Binstead.

Dell.R.F. – 1962 - **The Building of the County Hall, Lewes 1808-12** – Sussex Archaeological Society – Vol 100.

Downing.M&R. – March 2012 – **The Crouch**.

Elleray,D.Robert. - 1998 – ***A Millennium Encyclopaedia of Worthing History***

– Optimus Books Ltd.

Endacott, Sylvia – ***It Started with a Map*** – Sylvia Endacott.

Erredge.J.E. – 1862 – 1862 - ***History of Brighthelmston***.

Eustace.G.W. – ***Arundel: Borough & Castle*** – Robert Scott.

Furneaux.E.G. – 1955 - ***The Story of Polegate***.

Green, Alan HJ - 2007 - ***Georgian Chichester*** – Phillimore & Co Ltd.

Gregory, Albert.H. – 1933 - ***The Story of Burgess Hill*** – Charles Clarke.

Gwynne, Peter – 1990 - ***A History of Crawley*** – Phillimore & Co Ltd.

Hailsham Parish records 1850-98.

Hay, William. – 1804 – ***History of Chichester*** – J.Seagrave.

Hills, Wallace Henry - 1906 – ***History of East Grinstead*** – Farncombe & Co

Ltd.

Holloway, William. - 1845 – ***History & Antiquities of the Ancient Town & Port***

of Rye – John Russell Smith, London.

Houghton, John. – 1998– ***Unknown Lewes*** – Tartarus Press.

Hudson.T.P. – ***History of the County of Sussex-Vol 6 part 1: Bramber Rape***

(Southern Part).

Huggins, Dave - ***Memories of the old Town Hall.***

Kelly's Directory – Various editions.

Knight, Jeremy. – April 2012 – ***History of the Old Town Hall*** - article in AAH magazine.

Lambert, Tim - ***A History of Horsham***.

Leppard.M.J. – 2001 – ***A History of East Grinstead*** – Phillimore & Co Ltd.

Lewes District Council – 2004 – Conservation Area Appraisal Telscombe

Lewes, Seaford, Newhaven Directory. – Various editions.

Lower, Mark Antony. - 1870 – ***A Compendious History of Sussex – Vol I&II***

John Russell Smith, London.

MacDougall, Philip. - 2004 – ***The Story of Chichester*** – Sutton

Publishing.
- Manwaring Baines, J. – 1969 – **Historic Hastings** – F.J.Parsons Ltd.
- Middleton, Judy - 2013 – **Hove Town Hall**.
- Morgan, Roy. - 1992 – **Chichester A Documentary History** – Phillimore & Co Ltd.
- Murray, John. - 1858 – **Handbook Kent & Sussex**.
- National Archives – Various.
- Nemeth, Robert. - **Building Opinions**
- Odam, John - **Bygone Seaford** - Pdf
- Ogden, Peter – **Selsey Parish Council 1894-1945** – Selsey Society Publication
- Pennington, Janet – **The Market Houses of Steyning**. – Sussex Archaeological Collections.
- Parry, John D. – 1833 – **Historical & Descriptive Account of the Coast of Sussex.**
- Pikes Blue Book – Various.
- Poole, Helen. – 2000 – **Lewes Past** – Phillimore & Co Ltd.
- Porter, Julian. - 1998 – **Images of England, Bexhill-on-Sea**. – Tempus.
- Porter, Valerie. - 1994 – **The Village Parliaments** – Phillimore & Co Ltd.
- Robertson, Charles A. – 2005 - **Hailsham & its Environs** – Phillimore & Co Ltd.
- Rogers, Lilian. - 2002 – **Haywards Heath Past & Present** – S.B.Publications.
- Row, Ernest F. – 1913 – **A History of Midhurst Grammar School** – Combridge, Hove.
- Salzman, L.F. – 1953 - A History of the County of Sussex: Volume 4: The Rape of Chichester.
- Salzman, L.F. - 1940– **A History of the County of Sussex: Volume 7: The Rape of Lewes.**
- Short, B. (ed.), - '**A Very Improving Neighbourhood': Burgess Hill 1840-1914** (University of Sussex, Centre for Continuing Education Occasional Paper No. 23, 1984), 15.

Sickelmore, R. – 1827– **History of Brighton and its Environs**.
Surtees, John. – 2002 – **Eastbourne A History** –Phillimore & Co Ltd.
Taylor, Mary. – 2008 – **No 6, Origins of the Village Hall** – Print Plus, Arun
District Council.
Thornton, David. - 1987 – **Hastings: A Living History** - Hastings Publishing Co.
Turner, Rev Edward. – 1856– **The Early History of Brighton**.
Ward, Lock & Co. - 1901 – **Eastbourne.** (2nd edition).
White, Sally. – 2000 – **Worthing Past** – Phillimore & Co Ltd.
Wynter.W.R. – 1922 - **Old Seaford** – Farncombe & Co Ltd.
West Sussex Records Office – various council and parish minutes.
Anon - 1933 – **The Story of Crowborough** – Courier Co Ltd. Tunbridge Wells.
British Listed Buildings Online – various.

The Argus – 19 + 22 February 1999,18 December 2000,16 February 2011,11 June 2014.
Chichester Observer – 31 December 2008, 20 July 2014.
The London Gazette – various.
The Victoria History of the Counties of Sussex – Vol VI Part I - 1980
The Victoria History of the Counties of Sussex – Vol ll Part I – 1907.159.
The Comprehensive Gazetteer of England and Wales, 1894-5
Arun Gazette, 15 November 1985, 24 January, 8 August, 31 October 1986, 23 October 1987, 26 May 1989.
Bognor Regis Observer – various.
Eastbourne Chronicle – September 1889, 1890 & 1964 January/April.
East Grinstead Courier – 24 November 2011.
Hailsham Gazette – 27 October 2004.
Littlehampton Gazette news. Friday 7 May 2010.
Littlehampton Gazette news. 16 March 2000, 29 June 2013.
Shoreham Herald - 29 October 2014.
Sussex Express – 24 July 2001, 7 March 2003 and others.
Sussex Daily News – 29 April 1895. Plus others.
The Courier (Crowborough) – 8 June and 10 August 2012.
The Courier (Uckfield) – 26 July 1991. Plus others.

Bibliography

West Sussex County Times – 12 June 1936, 27 Oct 2009, 28 February, 10 April 2012.

West Sussex Gazette – 1 December 1958, 23 December 1982.

Worthing Herald & Gazette March 2013 articles by Ted Heasman.

Worthing Herald – June 2013.

Web Sites: http://www.abct.org.uk/airfields/polegate

www.theargus.co.uk/magazine/nostalgia/pastpresent/9818816.An_historic_hall/?ref=rss

www.bognor-local-history.co.uk/index-articles.html

www.burrows.co.uk/horshamguide/06Par.htm

http://217.204.55.158/henrymoore/sculptor/browserecord.php?-action=browse&-recid=2054

www.mybrightonandhove.org.uk

http://littlehamptonlifeboat.org.uk/station-history/

http://portsladehistory.blogspot.co.uk

http://en.wikipedia.org/wiki/User: Hassocks5489/B%26A_in_B%26H

www.stnicolas.standrewportslade.btinternet.co.uk/portslade_by_sea_history_pictures.htm

www.seafordtowncouncil.gov.uk/seaford.php

www.subbrit.org.uk/rsg/sites

http://www1.arun.gov.uk/cgi-bin/ptclerks.pl

www.workhouses.org.uk

http://www.nullens.org/sussex-arundel-houses/annex-2-mayors-arundel/#.U6VUzxZGV4M

'Arundel', ***A History of the County of Sussex: Volume 5 Part 1: Arundel Rape: Southwestern part, including Arundel*** (1997), pp. 10-101. URL: http://www.british-history.ac.uk/report.aspx?compid=22937. Date accessed: 11 August 2013.

http://www.british-history.ac.uk/report.aspx?compid=18257&strquery="fire station" Date accessed: 23 July 2014.

A P Baggs and H M Warne, 'Arundel', in ***A History of the County of Sussex:***

Volume 5 Part 1, Arundel Rape: South-Western Part,

 Including, ed.T.P.Hudson(London,1997) pp.10-101http://www.british-history.ac.uk/vch/sussex/vol5/- pt1/pp10-101[9 /6/15]

Lords to Bureaucrats

Biblography

Notes

The index is divided into two sections: 1. The first a list of people's names. 2. A general index covering all other matters. The bold page numbers indicate illustrations.

Index of People

Abraham, Robert, 23
Adams, Rev T.W., 151
Alard, jnr Gervase, 146, 148
Aldridge, Major John, 54
Andrews, John K., 88
    Thomas, 37
Ardagh, Lt John Charles, 162
Ashdown, Rt Hon Paddy, 33
Ashley, J.W.M., 156
Asquith, Mr, 167
Atherley, Arthur, 23
Aubrey-Fletcher, Sir Henry, 74

Baldwin, F, 163
Bannister, Thomas, 49
Barber, Horatio, 70
Barchard, Francis, 171
Barrie, J. M., 94
Bartholomew, Robert, 117
Bashford, William Charles Lake, 121
Baxter, Wynne Edwin, 127
Beal, Michael, 97
Bennett, Thomas, 45
Bennett-Stanford, Mrs Ellen, 121
Blackman, Frederick, 160
Blomfield, Sir Reginald, 132
Booker, John, 153

Booth, Mrs S, 77
Bosaquet, David Ives, 52
Boulton, Ald George, 112
Bowler, John, 29
    Thomas, 22
Braden, Cllr Hugh, 82
Bradford, James, 52
Brandon-Jones, J, 81
Brazell, Cllr David, 51
Bristow, John, 158
Brooks, W, 79
Brown, L. Capacity, 64
Browne, Sir Anthony, 62
Buckherste, Lord, 104
Bull, Robert, 40
Burfield, Thomas, 156
Burgeys family, 32
Burgoyne, Mrs, 52
Burningham, John, 59
Butlin, Billy, 28
Buttimer, Cllr Audrey, 124

Callaghan, Terry, 55
Callaway, Peter, 94
Campbell, C.A.M., 164
Cameron-Waller, Peter, 159
Campion, William, 133
Canning, George, 140
Catchpole, Jack, 134

183

Cavendish, Lord Edward, 112
Chalcraft, Mr, 76
Chamberlin, F, 70
Charles, Prince & Lady Diana, 139
Chappell, John Thomas, 109, 122
Chermayeff, Serge, 103
Chick, W. W., 50
Chignell, Marion Elizabeth, 68
Clark, Thomas Howe, 33
Clay, Cllr B, 44
Clayton, Mrs H. W., 96
    Newton, 96
Co, Henry, 33
Cockesbrayn, William, 117
Connolly, H, 114
Cooke, Charles, 163
Cooper, Maj. C.H., 169
    Thomas, 107
Cortlandt, Col Philip van, 158
    Brig Col Philip van, 158
Cortis, Alderman Alfred, 79
Cotmot, John, 133
Cowles-Voysey, Charles, 28, 81
Cowper, John, 131
Cramp, G.H., 151
Crane, Thomas, 23
Cranston, John, 87
Crawfurd, Rev Charles W Payne, 86
Cruttenden, Henry Edward, 117
Cutler, A. J. 96

Daly, Cllr E.J., 172
    Richard, 27
Daniel, Cllr Godfrey, 118
Denman, Samuel, 128
Dennett, W. H., 79
D.G. Jones, 118
Dickinson, General, 32

Dodins, Richard, 22
Donaldson, Group Cpt Teddy, 94
Doubleday, Mr., 107
Downer, W, 32
Drummond-Murray, Mrs, 89
Duffield, Ald. Harry Thomas, 81
Duchess of Kent, 134
Duchess of Gloucester, 154
DuGuay-Trouin, Rene, 110
Duke of Devonshire, 112
Duke, Sq Leader Neville, 94
Duke of Newcastle, 139
Duke of Norfolk, 23, 25, 54, 119
Duke of Richmond, 35 - 36
Duke & Duchess of York, 103
Duke, Thomas, 76
Durr, Andy, 106

Earl De La Warr, 102
Earl of Arundel, 104
Earl of Chichester, 131
Earl of Egremont, 64
Earl of Richmond, 38
Edes, John, 42
Edwardes-Jones, Reginald, 3
Elliot, Mr, 79
Emeleus, Cllr Robert, 151
Eversfield, Lord Charles, 53

Falkner, T, 158
Fanshawe, Simon, 106
Fawcett, Lt Col John, 107
Fitch, Cllr Brian & Mrs, 68
FitzAlan, Richard, E of Arundel, 22
Fleming, Ian, 89
Fletcher, Sir Henry, 71
Foden S.O., 139
Foulkes, William Tadman, 112
Fovargue, Cllr, 151

Index of People

Fowler, Frederick Bernard, 110 - 111
    John, 38
Francis, Sir Frank, 115
Freshfield, Dr Edwin, 147
Fuller, John, 110
Fryer, W.J., 102

Gardiner, William, 74
Gates, J. Percy, 54
George, Prince, D of Kent. 81
Gibbon, Philips, 139
Gordon-Lennox, Charles, D of Richmond, 35, 41
Gorham, Ambrose, 169
Goring, George, 133
Gott, Peter, 117
Gould, Sir N, 70
Grice, William, 29
Guy, David, 159

Haine, John, 111
Hales, Charles, 50
Hall, Cllr A.J., 171
    John, 74
Hammond, John, 150
Hancock, R. S., 40
Hanham, Gilbert, 62
Harker, William Henry, 71
Harman, James Ambrose, 169
Harmer, Ron, 159
Harris, Arthur C, 39
Harvey, Rev Francis Clyde, 156
Hay, Thomas, 116
Heasman, A., 93
Her Grace Lavinia, Duchess of Norfolk, 82
Hide, Charles, 80
Hillman, Edward, 128
Holland, Laurie, 142

Hollis, Cllr Geoffrey J., 90
Holman, T. Jeffrey, 159
Holmes, James, 25
Holmes, Lillian May, 24
Holmwood, G, 114
Honisett, C.J., 151
Hooper, George Henry, 71
Hotham, Sir Richard, 26, 29
Houlgate, David, 68
Howard, Bernard D of Norfolk, 23
    Andrew, 66
    Henry Charles D of Norfolk, 53
    Ebenezer, 102
    Edward, 23
Howlett, Alderman James Warnes, 122 - 123
Huchs, Frank, 111
Hudson, Ald. Alice, 114
Huggett, Mrs Jean D, 66
Hurdis, James, 144
Hurst, Robert Henry, 52, 54, 56 – 57
Hurst, Col. A.R., 57
Huntbach, Barry, 68

Ingram, Arthur, 53
Ingram, Col, 76
Irwin, Lord & Lady, 54

Jelf, Andrew, 139
Johnson, J. J., 38
    John, 126, 131
Jones, Cllr Anne, 33
    D.G. 118
    Ralph, 79
Jubb, Joseph, 29

Keen, David, 58
Kemp, Thomas Read, 107
    Mr, 165
Kempthorne, Sampson, 164
Kendall, H.E., 170
King, Stephen, 49
Knifton, Mrs Rebecca, 66
Knight, E. W., 63
Knott, John, 35
Knowles, Sir James, 109

Laker, Eric George, 89
Lamb, James, 139
Lane, Lt Col Henry, 100 - 101
Langridge, William Balcombe, 131
Lascelles, Col H.A., 61
Lemon, Mark, 45
Lennox, Charles, Duke of Richmond, 35, 41
Leonard, Mrs Alma., 95
Lewes, Brandon, 82
Lintill, Ken, 66
Lintott, William, 54
Lister, Major J, 49
Little, Cllr Sydney, 72
Lock, Lt, 167
Long, A. T., 27
Long, Martyn, 83
Lyons, Fred, 94

MacCleod, Capt. Norman A, 55
McIndoe, Sir Archie, 86
McWilliam, Geoffrey, 91
Mant, Arthur French, 65
Mardell, John Whitly, 70
Marquess of Abergavenny, 155
May, Francis, 108
    R, 44
Meads, J. 32

Mears, Thomas, 80
Mendelsohn, Eric, 103
Merrick, Joseph Carey, 127
Michell, John, 57
Miles, William, 132
Miller, Mr, 159
    Sir John, 35 – 36
Mitchell, William George, 134
Milward, Edward, 117
Monk-Bretton, Lord, 3, 114, 130
Moore, John, 117
Montfort, Simon de, 8
Montgomery, Roger de, 22
Morris, John, 126
    Sir John, 139
    Roger, 36
Murphy, Lt Col C.C.R., 89
Mursell, Sir Peter, 42

Nevill, Lord Rupert, 124
Neville, Charles William, 165, 169
Newell, Betty, 91

Ockenden, John, 140

Packham, William H, 61
Pannett, Richard, 49
    Arthur Richard, 49
Parker, H.W., 139
Parry, Sir Hubert., 94
Parsons, Latter, Mr, 132
Payne, Anthony S., 166
Peck, Frederick, 87
Peckham, Henry 'Lisbon" and Elizabeth, 38
Peerless, James, 112
Pelham, Family, 133
    Henry, 140
    James, 117
    Thomas, 133

Index of People

Pinchin, C.D., 94
Pitt, William, The Elder, 140
Poole, Family 71
    William Sandford, 50
Potter, Joseph, 54
Pratten, Mrs Molly E., 169
Prince of Wales, 106
Puggesley, Clement, 125
Pullinger, Colin, 97
    Charles, 97
Pultney, John, 117

Rakele, Henry de, 137
Raper, W.A., 150
Rayner, Frederick J., 163
Redman, Willam Jupp, 25
Reeve, K, 139
Reeves, William H., 118
Renals, Sir Joseph, 102
Revill, Ald. W.F., 119
Ridley, Nicholas, 91
Robbins, Chris, 24
Roberts, Dr Isaac, 171
Rose, Charles, 67
Roth, Stanley, 43
Rouen, Emery De, 33
Rowe, Cllr Mrs Arlene, 155
Russell, Dr Richard, 105
    Mr., 121

Sackville, Reginald Windsor, Earl De La Warr, 101
Sacre, Mrs E, 29
    Rev Canon A. J., 29
Scrase, A. P., 32
Scott, Paul, 94
    Paul D, 154
Scutt, Ken, 30
Searle, H.R., 155, 157, 161
Serigson, Family, 52

    Rev William, 46
Serigson, Thomas, 128
Seymour, H.W., 29
Shanks, Michael, 166
Shelley, Sir Timothy, 79
Shields, Robert, 68
Simpson, Gilbert, 68
    Mr, 110
Sinnock, H.C., 158
Sly, Mrs, 158
Smart, Henry, 38
Smirke, Sydney, 71
Smith, Family, 57, 62
    J, 94
    Jim G, 44
    W.J., 127
Speed, Bert, 66
Squires, Anthony H., 90
Stenning, W.V.K., 87
Stewart, Rt. Hon Michael, 48
Stewart-Roberts, Phyllida, 145
Stillman, C. G., 43
Stinchcombe, Mrs Pat, 29
Stone, George, 163
Stonestreet, Benjamin, 160
Streatfield, R.S., 170
Strickland, William, 158
    Mrs, 158
Stringfellow, Mr, 27
Stone, Andrew, 117
Strong, Joan Vera, 89
Swinton, Lord, 45

Tankard, Cllr Ian, 167
Tettersel, Nicholas, 69
Thatcher, Frederick, 151
Thomas, Charles, 101
Thomas-Atkin, Chris, 33
Treacher, Mr, 52
Tress, William, 150

Tuck, Buckmaster Joseph, 144
Tullett, George E, 34

Ushsher, Charles W Neville, 165

Verger, E. A., 132
Verrall, George, 126
Vulliamy, Benjamin, 80

Waleys, Henry de, 146
Wallis, George Ambrose, 113
Ward, Henry, 101 – 102, 118
Warr, George Walter, 74
Warenne, Rainard de, 125
Waterhouse, Alfred, 121
Webb, Sidney & Beatrice, 5
Wells-Thorpe, John, 124
West, C, 165
Wheeler, Robert, 170
White, T. H., 3
Whitehouse, Graham, 25
Wicker, John, (Lord Nutham) 57
Widgery, Lord, 119
Wilds, Amon, 126
Williams, Margaret Lister, 52
       R, 114
Willis, Henry, 123
      R. B., 3, 41
Wilson, Sir Colin Alexander
  St John, 39
Winter, Henry, 119
Wolfe, Miss, 153
       General James, 153
Woodman, Richard, 77
Woodruff, George B, 120
Woolacott, R. J., 50
Wonham, W. K., 27
Wyatt, James, 37
Wyndham, John, 65

Yarrow, Cllr R.H., 129

General Index

A & J Mighell, 51
Airfields, ALG, 29, 45, 70, 93,
  110 - 111, 167
Albion House, 51
Ambulance Service
  5, 24, 32, 41, 65, 119
  St John Service, 24, 41, 74
  Red Cross, 27, 41
Architects & Surveyors, 11
  W.Sx.
    23 - 25, **27** - 28, 36 - 37, 39,
    40, 43, 45, 47, 49, 54, 56, 60,
    68, 71, 74, 78 – 79, 81 - 82,
    87, 91, 94
  E. Sx,
    101 - 103, 107 – 109, 112
    114, 118, 121, 124 -125, 129,
    131 - 133, 138, 150 – 151, 155,
    162 – 164, 169 - 170
Arts Council, 39
Arundel Improvement Act 1785,
  23

Barracks see under Forts.
Bartholomew House, 108
BLB Group, 128
Bohemia House, 119
Brewer Smith & Brewer, 94
Brian Sellars Associates, 169
Brick/Tile Works, 31, 43, 93, 166
Brighton Town Act 1825, 105
Broadfield House, 45 – 47, **46**
Broadfield Park, 46
Brodie Plant Goddard, 60
Brunswick Square and BrunswickTerrace Improvement Act 1830, 120
Brussels Town Hall, 9

Builders,
  W. Sx, 27, 29, 32, 37 - 38, 40, 46
    47, 49, 51, 54, 58, 60, 71, 76,
    78, 79, 81 - 82, 87, 91, 94
  E. Sx, 101 - 102, 107, 109, 112,
    114, 116, 118, 120 – 121, 125,
    127, 131 - 133, 158, 160, 163,
    171
Butler & Son (London), 79
Butlin, Billy, 28

Capron House, 63
Castlegate House, 131
Celtic, 7, 110, 135
Centenary House, 42, 83
Charity Commission, 63, 136-137
Charter of Incorporation, 47,
  100, 102, 104, 107, 111, 113,
  114 – 116, 120, 127, 140
Chichester Chancel, **34**
Cinque Ports Association, 2 - 3,
  115, 135, 137 - 138, 140, 146
City Council, 99;
  Brighton, 109;
  Chichester, 34, 37;
  Worthing, 85
Civic centres, 11, 26, **72**, 72, 91 –
  92, **91,** 120, **168,** 169, 171 – 172
Civil defence, 11,133
Clarke Roofing Southern Ltd,
  128
Clocks, 8, 29 - 30, 54 - 55, 65, 74,
  80, 82, 104, 112 - 113, 115,
  117, 122
Coast Guard, 78, 110, 120
Coldstream House, 142
Comewell House, 56
Conder Projects, 91

Co-operative Estates Company, 166
Coade & Sealey, 132
Corporations, 4, 6, 9;
 Arundel, 23; Brighton, 104;
 Chichester, 33, 35 - 37;
 Crawley, 45 – 47;
 Eastbourne, 110 - 111, 115;
 Hastings 115, 117; Hove, 120;
 Pevensey 2, 136;
 Rye, 137 - 139; Seaford, 140;
 Winchelsea, 146
Corporation Reform Act
 1832, 2, 86; Reform Act 1835, 33
Cortlandt House,
 157 - 158, **157**, 161
  Property LLP, 158
Council House, **36**
Councils see County council, District council, Town council, Parish council.
County Boroughs, 19, 61, 70, 79, 86;
 Arundel, 22, 25, 91;
 Brighton, 2 - 3, 104, 107, 169;
 Bexhill, 100, 102- 103,151;
 Chichester, 33, 42; Crawley, 44;
 Eastbourne, 2- 3, 111, 114 - 115;
 Hastings 2 - 3, 103, 116, 119 – 120;
 Horsham, 52; Hove, 68;
 Lewes, 124, 126 – 129, 142;
 Rye, 137 -138, 151; Seaford, 140;
 Steyning, 75; Worthing, 82 - 83
County Councils, 2, 9, 21, 99;
 W.Sx, 3, 24, 30, 41, 51, - 52, 60, 63, 65 - 66, 76 - 77, 83, 86, 88, 90, 95, 97
 E.Sx, 3, 49, 99, 103, 107, 114, 129– 133, 139, 142, 145, 149, 152 – 153, 155, 166, 168
County Hall, 42, **43**, 130 - 134, **131**, **134**
County Hall North, 52, 60, **60**
Court Leet, 7, 11
Courts, 4, 8, 10 – 12;
 W. Sx. 23 - 25, 33, 35, 37 - 38, 47, 53, 55, 62, 76, 80 - 81, 86
 Courts... E. Sx. 104, 113, 118 - 119, 125, 130 - 132, 140, 146 – 147, 150
Crickmay of Horsham, 55
Critchell Harrington (Chichester), 82
Crompton & Co, 122

Davis Coffer Lyons, 55
De La Warr Pavilion, 103
District Councils, 2;
 Adur, 3, 71 - 72, 74,82;
 Arun, 3, 25 – 26, 29 - 30, 90 - 92, 94 – 95;
 Arundel, 25 - 26; Battle, 103;
 Chichester, 38,40, 61, 63, 66, 97;
 Crawley, 3; Eastbourne, 3;
 Hailsham, 159; Hastings, 3;
 Horsham, 3, 57 – 59 - 60, 77;
 Lewes, 128 - 129, 142 - 143, 145, 149, 162, 163 - 164;
 Mid-Sussex, 3, 32, 41, 51 - 52, 86, 88; Newhaven, 166;
 Rother 3, 103, 139, 146, 149, 151;
 Rye, 139; Shoreham, 74:
 Southwick, 74;
 Wealden 3, 137, 149, 154 - 155, 157 – 159, 161, 167 – 168, 172;
 Worthing, 3;
Divided Parishes Act 1882, 146
Downford House, 158
Durban House, 30, 42

General Index

Eastbourne Corporation Act
    1910, 114
Eastbourne Flying School, 111
East Court, **87**, 87
East Pallant House, **40,** 40
East Sussex Review Order 1934,
    114
ECE Architecture, 82, 129
Emergency Centres, 11, 29, 44,
    48, 59, 133
English Heritage, 65

Ferries, 69, 89, 104, 163
Fitzroy Robinson Miller Bourne
    & Partners, 109
Fire, 5, 58, 89, 108, 122 - 123, 140,
    145, 160;
  Appliances, 4, 9, 24, 32, 54, 62 –
    63, 65, 75, 80, 96, 102, 108,
    113-114, 117 - 118, 151, 160, 164;
  Brigades, 9, 25, 32, 65, 75, 80, 96,
    108, 136, 139;
  Stations 4, 49, 62, 67, 71, 94, 96,
    102, 114, 119, 145, 153, 156,
    160, 164;
  Volunteers 9, 24, 27, 32, 45, 49,
    54, 62, 80, 96, 113, 117 - 118,
    153
FitzAlan, Chapel, 23
Fitzgerald Charity, 144
Forts/Barracks, 44, 70, 93, 100,
    134, 156, 162
Foundation Stones, 84, 148
Frankham Consultancy Group
    Ltd, 162
Frank Hucks Waterplane
    Company, 111

Gas & Electricity, 24, 33, 76, 169,
    127, 195 – 196
Gates Brewery, 77
Gillett & Bland, 122
Gillett & Johnson, 82, 112, 123
Good & Kay, 56
Gotch & Partners, 124
Grey Friars, 34
Guildbourne Centre, 80

Hall & Co, 80
HNW, 40
Hope Brewery, 86
Horsham Building Society, 54
Hove Improvement Act 1858, 120
Hubbard Ford Partnership, 155
Humphreys Ltd, 47
HMS Lizard, 109
Hundreds, 2, 8, 13 – 18
  W.SX, 22, 26, 31, 33, 44, 52, 61,
    64, 67, 69, 73, 78, 86, 88, 93, 95
  E. SX, 100, 104, 110, 115, 120,
    137, 140, 146, 150, 153, 156,
    162, 168, 170
Hurdis House, 141, 143, **144**
H.W. Seymour, 29

Individual Service Builders, 94
Inglenook, 158 - 159, **159**
Inns & Hotels,
  Angel, 62; Bell, 100; Castle, 105;
  Chequer, 75; Crown, 156;
  George, 150, 156;
  Kings Head, 156;
  Maiden's Head, 170; Nelson, 78;
  Old Ship, 105; Prince's, 109;
  Railway, 32; Royal George, 78;
  Ship, 120; Smugglers, 135;
  Star, 127, 150; Station, 49;
  Swan, 35; Terminus, 156, 160;
  White Hart, 125 - 126;

White Horse, 75
J. Lawson & Co Ltd, 134
James Linfield & Sons Ltd., 94
James Longley & Co Ltd, 46, 58
Jane Penfold Institute, 76
John Edes House, 41 - 43, **42**,

Keepmoat Ltd, 115
Keith Andrews & Co, 82
Kier Ltd, 166
Kings House, **109**
Kingsley Eco Solutions, 92

Leconhall, Estate, 65
    Hall Trust, 65
Lewes House, 129, 133
Libraries, 10 – 11, 39, 42, 58, 82,
    111, 114 - 115, 118, 153, 155,
    166, 170
Lifeboats, 70, 78, 89, 96, 110, 120,
    137, 162
Lighthouse, 110
Lighting & Watching Act 1833,
    4, 52
Listed Buildings, 4, 11, 115;
  W. SX, Grade I, 35, 43
    Grade II, 23, 29 - 30, 38, 40, 46,
      55, 57, 63, 65, 71, 76, 82, 87, 90
  E.SX, Grade I, 106, 147
    Grade II, 108 – 109, 113, 118 –
      119, 121, 128, 133, 141,
      150, 152, 158, 160
Lloyds of London, 162
Local Board, see under
individual town entries.
Local Govt Acts,
    1848, 89;   1858, 70, 111;
    1888, 2, 33, 99, 107, 130;
    1894, 10, 27, 56, 65, 87, 101, 116,
      120, 163;

    1929, 49;
Local Govt Acts,
    1972, 3, 11, 32, 34, 40, 44, 82,
      103, 116, 129, 151, 157, 161;
    1974, 38, 68;   1997, 10
Local Government Order 1910,
    71
Local Government & Rating Act
    1997, 10
London Carriage Company, 46
Long and Kentish, 39

Maidiment's Garage, 96
Manor House, 74, 89 - 91, 90**,**
    105, 106
Martello Tower, 139
Mayors, 4, 6, 11;
  W Sx 3, 22 – 26, 29, 33 - 35, 37, 40,
    44, 50, 59, 63, 68, 70, 75, 79,
    81 – 83, 85, 88, 90 – 91, 94 - 95
  E. Sx, 100, 102, 106, 112 - 116,
    117, 119 - 120, 124, 128,
    137, 139, 142, 146 – 149,
    151, 154, 159, 164, 166
    167, 169, 171 - 172
Members of Parliament, 3, 23, 26,
    33, 41, 48, 52 - 54, 56 - 57, 74,
    82, 91, 104, 107, 110, 117, 133,
    139
Meridian Centre, **165,** 166
Michell & Thyne, 68
Millennium, 29, 106
Monarchs,
  Alfred, 22;
  Charles II, 69; Edgar, 33, 168;
  Edward the Confessor 2;
  Edward I, 8, 146;
  Edward II, 104; Edward III, 8;
  Edward VII, 100, 142;
  Elizabeth I, 22, 116, 119;

General Index

Elizabeth II, 45; George II, 37;
Monarchs,
  George V, 26; Harold, 119;
  Henry I, 150; Henry III, 135, 156;
  Henry VIII, 34, 89, 127, 140;
  James II, 33; John, 69, 70, 136;
  Offa, 100; Stephen, 33, 125, 136;
  Victoria, 79;
  William I, 95, 115, 119, 135, 150;
  William III, 64
Motor Racing, 100, 103
Municipal Corporation Act 1835,
  6, 23;
  1882, 61, 113; 1883, 136, 146
Municipal Reform Act 1835, 4, 9,
Museums, 4, 11, 25, 82, 90, 108,
  118, 123, 140, 147, 152

National Fire Service, 9, 32, 74
National/Heritage Lottery,
  25, 39, 65, 90, 106, 118
New Anzac on Sea, 165
NewHouse, 158
New Park House, **58**, 58
New Towns Act 1946, 45

Oaklands, 50 – 52, 51
Old Abbey Gate House, 150
Operation Hadrian, 29

Pallant House, 38, **39**, 40
Pallant House Gallery, 39
C & C. J. Pannett, 132
Parish Act, 1878, 93; 1894, 2
Parish Councils, 2, 5, 9 - 10, 13 –
  18, 42, 51, 66, 71, 73, 75,
  77, 85, 91, 93 - 97, 103, 135
  136-137, 142, 149, 151, 153 - 154,
  156, 157 – 159, 161, 166– 169
Park House, 55, **57,** 57,

Park North, **59,**
Parkside, 42, 60
Parliament, 8, 23, 45, 78
Parliament Act 1822, 27
Peck and Stevens, 87
Pelham House, 130 - 134, **133,**
Pellings LLP, 115
Personal Travel Service, 158
Petworth House, 64
Pine Grove, 154, 155, 161 - 162
Police, 5, 6, 24, 41, 74, 83, 105, 113,
  125, 164;
  Stations, 4, 10, 32, 47, 54, 108,
    113, 118 - 119, 121 - 122, 145;
  Fire, 108, 121 - 122
Poor Law Act 1834, 9, 111
Poor Relief Act 1601, 9
Pope Building Services, 40
Portland House, 72 - 73, 82, 84
Priory House, 108
Prospect House, 161
Public Loan Board, 169

Quarter sessions, 5, 23, 35, 55,
  131 - 132, 139

Radio Mercury, 47
RAF, 45, 86,
Raids, 1 - 2, 119;   Air 139;
  French 1-2, 104, 115, 138, 146;
  Danish 1; Norman 1;
  Roman 2;   Spanish 1, 146
Railway, 12, 32, 34, 48, 67, 70, 74,
  78, 86, 93, 96, 106, 110,
  140, 156, 163, 166
  Stations, 24, 27, 32, 45, 62, 64,
    75, 89, 103, 125, 136, 148, 150,
    153, 167
Rapes, 2, 7, 13 - 18, 21;
  W.SX, 22, 26, 32 - 33, 41, 44, 52, 61

64, 67, 69, 73, 75, 78, 86, 88, 93, 95.
Rapes,
   E. SX, 99 - 100, 104, 110, 115, 120,
      125, 135, 137, 140, 146, 150,
      153, 156, 162, 168, 170
Real Land Ltd, 158
Representation of the People Act
   1867, 12
Ronuk Hall, 68
      Polish Factory, 67
Royal Exchange Assurance
   Company, 160
Royal Navy, 69, 105, 111
Royal Pavilion, 106, 108
Rugby Securities Holdings Ltd,
   166
Rural District Councils,
   10 - 11, 19 – 20;
   Battle 3, 117, 138, 151;
   Chailey, 129, 142, 166;
   Chichester, 34, 39 – 40, 91, 97;
   Chanctonbury, 52, 59, 78;
   Cuckfield, 44, 49, 51 – 52;
   Eastbourne, 114;
   East Grinstead, 87;
   Hailsham, 3, 114, 155 - 158, 161,
      167, 172; Hastings, 117;
   Haywards Heath, 49;
   Horsham, 44, 52, 56, 59;
   Midhurst, 34, 38, 61 - 63;
   Newhaven, 164;
   Petworth, 34, 38, 65;
   Rye, 160; Steyning, 78;
   Uckfield 3, 155, 157, 161, 170 – 172;
   Westhampnett, 38 - 39, 97;
   Worthing, 80, 91
Rural Sanitary Authority 1872,
      61, 65

Salviati, Burke & Co, 122
Saxons, 1, 8, 44, 61, 73, 75, 86, 88,
   104, 115, 124, 135, 145, 162
Schools,
   Bognor, Jubilee, 27;
   Crawley, West Green County
   Junior, 46 Discovery Free, 47;
   Hailsham, Infants, 156;
   Hastings, Summerfields, 119;
   Midhurst Grammar, 62;
   Portslade, St Andrews, 67;
   Seaford, Downs, 143;
   Selsey, Infants, National,
   Medmerry Academy, Seal
      Academy, 96;
   Shoreham, National, 70;
   Steyning, National, 75, Infants,
      76
Sheep/ Cattle fairs, 31, 48, 156
Sir John Brown & Henson, 47
Smith of Derby, 29
South Coast Land & Resort Co,
   169
Southdown Motor Company, 28
South East Electricity Board, 109
Southover House, **129,** 129
St Andrews Hall, 77
Stained Glass Windows, 10, 49,
   112, 119
Starfield, 155, 161, 170 - 171
Stanford Estate, 109, 121
Szerelmey Ltd, Messrs, 132

Technical Institute, 111, 114
The Almonry, 151, **152,**
The Broadway, **154,**
The Crouch, 142
The Hunt Partnership, 38
The Steyning Centre, **77,** 77
The Steyning Public Hall &

General Index

Assembly Co, 76
Town Act 1806, 125
Town Councils, 3, 11;
  W. SX, Arundel, 23, 25 – 26;
  Bognor, 26 - 29;
  Burgess Hill, 32 – 33;
  East Grinstead, 87 – 88;
  Haywards Heath, 50 – 51;
  Littlehampton, 90 -91;
  Midhurst, 63; Petworth, 66;
  Rustington, 94 – 95;
  Selsey, 96 – 97;
  Worthing, 79 – 80, 85
  E. SX, 149;
  Battle, 151 – 152; Bexhill, 103;
  Crowborough, 153 – 154;
  Eastbourne, 112;
  Hailsham, 157 – 161;
  Hastings, 117; Lewes, 125, 128;
  Peacehaven, 166;
  Polegate, 167 – 168; Rye, 139;
  Seaford, 142 – 145;
  Telscombe, 169; Uckfield, 171
Town Halls see under individual town entries.
Towns Police Act 1847, 9
Town Trusts, 63, 103, 136 - 137
Trollope & Colls Ltd, 81
Tunmore Design and Build, 26

Urban Councils, 4, 10 - 11, 19 – 20;
  W. SX. Bognor, 27, 91;
  Burgess Hill, 32, 41, 51;
  Crawley, 44;
  Cuckfield, 41, 49 - 52;
  E Grinstead, 41, 51, 86 - 87;
  Hayward Heath, 49 – 50;
  Horsham, 52, 54 – 55, 57;
  Littlehampton, 89, 91;
  Portslade, 67; Shoreham, 71 – 72

  Southwick, 71 - 74
Urban Councils,
  E. SX. Bexhill, 101;
  Battle, 150; Hove, 120;
  Newhaven, 129, 142, 163 – 164;
  Seaford, 129, 142 - 143;
  Uckfield, 170 - 171

Vestry, 4, 5, 9 - 10, 75, 100, 105, 156, 160
Votes, 5-6, 9, 12

Walter Llewellyn & Sons, 114, 124
Watching & Lighting Act 1835, 9
Wates Group Ltd, 60
Wealden Lodge, 171
West Sussex Review Order 1933, 80
W. H. Bailey, of Manchester, 54
W. H. Saunders & Son., 91
Winchelsea, **147**
William Mercer & Son, 62
Willmot Dixon Construction, 155, 162
Woodlands Centre, **93**, 94
Workhouse, 38, 61, 87, 105, 114, 150, 156, 159, 164, 170
Worthing Town Improvement Act 1803, 78

ABOUT THE AUTHOR

Stephen was born in North London in 1944 and schooled in Hove, Sussex and London with a special interest in History and Geography. After many years in the travel industry setting up and managing new branches for a large tour operator, he started his own business within the retail trade. As a life long philatelist, Stephen later moved to Eastbourne, East Sussex in 1985, and operated an online and retail stamp shop. Writing poetry and short stories, rekindled an interest in history and Sussex.

Stephen is working on a second book about a local Napoleonic barrack in Sussex and researching another historical book about an American loyalist living in England.

www.ingramcontent.com/pod-product-compliance
Lightning Source LLC
Chambersburg PA
CBHW060520100426
42743CB00009B/1393